THE NEW WORLD ORDER, ARMAGEDDON, AND BEYOND

CHARLES POPE

Copyright © 2023 by Charles Pope.

ISBN: 979-8-89090-158-3 (sc)

All rights reserved. No part of this book may be reproduced or transmitted in any form or by any means, electronic or mechanical, including photocopying, recording, or by any information storage and retrieval system, without permission in writing from the copyright owner.

The views expressed in this work are solely those of the author and do not necessarily reflect the views of the publisher, and the publisher hereby disclaims any responsibility for them.

EXPRESSO
Executive Center 777, Dunsmuir Street Vancouver, BC V71K4
1-888-721-0662 ext 101
info@expressopublishing.com

TABLE OF CONTENTS

Chapter 1　Foundational background information 25

Chapter 2　God's religious system and government for israel the foundational footprint of the plan of god for mankind 48

Chapter 3　The ancient kingdoms of mankind 64

Chapter 4　False prophet/beast power and new world order 100

Chapter 5　Exploring The "Latter Days" Prophesies 117

Chapter 6　Seals Five, Six and Seven 132

Chapter 7　Armageddon and the kingdom of god 152

PREFACE

This book is years ahead of its time. Nevertheless, it has information that is not well known in historic or religious circles. The content is very deep, and I advise you to read it slowly and perhaps one chapter at a sitting. I say this because the information requires mental thought and spiritual reasoning.

There are many books about the coming Apocalypse and God destroying the power of evil at the end of the world. There is not one book out there **with this information** and background to substantiate the possibilities. This book is not just about *"doom and gloom."* There is a positive outcome of world peace and prosperity for mankind in the "endgame." However, we are living in dangerous times. Global threats of terrorism are an everyday issue. The possibility of a nuclear bomb in the hands of despots and unreasonable dictators is a reality. Iran, Korea, Syria, Russia, and China are legitimate concerns for the freedom loving nations of the world.

The political and economic demise of America is moving closer to a **losing position** as the leader of the free world. We are now in a battle for the minds and hearts of common-sense leadership to help the people of America survive the corruption, like a cancer slowly eroding what the forefathers intended as foundational order for this country.

Is the new administration of American government allowing the stage to be set for a New World Order for the nations? The proposed new trade policies with other nations are a clear path to upset nations. How can we as a nation, with the largest national debt ever accumulated, bring peace and posterity for all nations? Will there be a national system of government and treasure rise from Europe establishing a new world order for the nations? It is a fact, other nations such as China, Japan, and Germany; once our enemies, are now years ahead of America in wealth, technology, and infra-structure. America is operating with a crumbling infra-structure and a huge national debt to these nations.

Just today, an announcement of the United States Embassy will officially be moved to Jerusalem. We are now telling the world that Israel has the right as a sovereign nation to make Jerusalem the legitimate capital of Israel. This has stirred up the anger of the Palestinians, (ancient Philistines) to continue their claim to what God gave Israel as their inheritance.

People have forgotten this problem began in 1948 when the League of Nations accepted Israel as a state. This conflict has existed for centuries dating back to David and Goliath. The Palestinians are the ancient Philistines. A fact of history many do not know.

Most anyone you ask; believes we are living in the end-times of what the bible predicts will become the Great Tribulation and Armageddon.

What you are about to read is the most comprehensive information attached to the central themes of the book of Daniel and Revelation concerning events that are prophesied to occur in the end-times.

The bible is the reliable source for information just ahead in our future. Its prophesies have proven to be accurate time after time in history. It predicts the demise of nations; unless the nations as a people return to the God of their fathers and stop compromising and placating to people who do not practice the principles God.

Many people do not realize that the bible is a book about world governments. Beginning in the time of Daniel the prophet, God began to reveal world empires and governments that will influence the behavior of humanity until the end of time on earth. Jesus came to reveal a better way of life for all of humanity. His main purpose was to provide salvation for all who would believe in Him. He also preached about His coming world government that will provide what mankind's governments cannot accomplish, world peace.

Most of the principles the Founding Fathers for this nation are of biblical origin and have disappeared. Justice has fallen in the streets. Two standards of justice are active in the Supreme halls of Justice. People are obsessed with issues from that past, while the rest of the world is preparing their nations to be part of a New World Order. We as a nation are on the precipice of a cliff that will cause us to fall into an abyss of economic chaos as the leader of the world nations.

America Has Lost Its Moral Compass

Part of the problem is most Americans, especially *"Christians"* do not know what the bible says about world government and being a good steward of financial and physical blessings. These things start with the individual morals and actions of a nation's people. Their preachers tell their believers *what they want to hear*. It is not that *"old time religion"* it is the *"feel good about yourself religion."* I personally think the preachers and teachers in today's churches owe their members an apology. They are not preparing their members for the coming Kingdom of God to this earth. If they understood Christ is coming here and they are responsible to be prepared while living a moral life till He comes back; it would be effective. The teachings of Jesus and the Apostles is "hijacked" less than one hundred years after they are crucified and murdered. Think I am crazy? Count the churches, the prisons, and jails in cities. The *"Gospel of Jesus Christ and the Apostles"* has been reduced to believing *"once saved always saved"* with a *halo* and a *rocking chair* for salvation; or an ever-burning hell where people are writhing and screaming with torture forever. This conceptual doctrine is from 3rd and 4th century ideas, of men teaching *"fear religion"*.

Constantine, whom the world mistakenly calls the **"Father of Christianity"** is a **"wolf in sheep's clothing."** They do not see the truth of Constantine's claim of Christian conversion was for political purposes, not heartfelt repentance, and conversion to the way of Christ. He was using carnal reasoning to solve a problem by using religion as His flag of opportunity.

The coming **Kingdom of God** or **Prophecy** is rarely a topic in churches. Churches should be teaching and preparing people for the coming economic crisis, a New World Order and The Great Tribulation. Jesus came to earth to teach things that prepare us to be *"first responders"* in His Kingdom. The bible says Christ is coming here to the earth! Christ is coming back to judge and make war on the wickedness of humanity and the governments of men.

The thousands of religious people wear *"Christianity,"* as a badge. They settle for *"spoon-fed"* ideologies to soothe their conscience. They seldom study their bible and search out the truth about their destiny. These people fill football stadiums and are taught a *"carnal self-help."* They do not understand the Holy Spirit as the power of God in us that can transform our lives. The pre-digested 3rd and 4th century thinking of churches is a major cancer in the modern churches of today. [2]They have no clue what the Apostle Paul meant by the *"mystery of the gospel."* [3]I blame this problem on the preachers and teachers, not the people who go to churches to hear the

---

[1] Revelation 19:17-21

(17) And I saw an angel standing in the sun; and he cried with a loud voice, saying to all the fowls that fly during heaven, Come, and gather yourselves together unto the supper of the great God.

(18) That ye may eat the flesh of kings, and the flesh of captains, and the flesh of mighty men, and the flesh of horses, and of them that sit on them, and the flesh of all men, both free and bond, both small and great.

(19) And I saw the beast, and the kings of the earth, and their armies, gathered to make war against him that sat on the horse, and against his army.

(20) And the beast was taken, and with him the false prophet that wrought miracles before him, with which he deceived them that had received the mark of the beast, and them that worshipped his image. These both were cast alive into a lake of fire burning with brimstone.

(21) And the remnant was slain with the sword of him that sat upon the horse, which sword proceeded out of his mouth: and all the fowls were filled with their flesh.

[2] Col 1:26-27

(26) Even the mystery which hath been hid from ages and from generations, but now is made manifest to his saints:

(27) To whom God would make known what the riches of the glory of this mystery is among the Gentiles, **which is Christ in you,** *the hope of glory:*

[3] Ezekiel 34:1-3

(1) And the word of the LORD came unto me, saying,

(2) Son of man, prophesy against the shepherds of Israel, prophesy, and say unto them, thus says the Lord GOD unto the shepherds; Woe be to the shepherds of Israel that do feed themselves! should not the shepherds feed the flocks?

(3) Ye eat the fat, and ye clothe you with the wool, ye kill them that are fed: but ye feed not the flock.

gospel and are taught the 3rd and 4th century information of Constantine, a known pagan anarchist. They do not live their Christianity as a personal relationship with Christ, through the Holy Spirit. Too much emphasis on church social order and not enough bible study for understanding. The bible is about government and moral living as a people.

The condemnation falls upon the leadership of religions and churches when they **do not** teach the true Gospel of Jesus Christ to the people. The Gospel includes government and national morality. Churches that have much of the truth of God [4] continue year after year to be the *"guardian of the ashes"* that was the Old Covenant God made with ancient Israel. They lack *"keeping alive the fire"* by annual rituals and not letting the Holy Spirit motivate their daily lives as witnesses to the world. They become cliques of people who think they are *"one-up"* on the world of churches in their understanding. They splinter into hundreds of little island groups trying to tell others how they have the truth.

Korea is an example of bad government. The current North Korean dictator threatening nuclear war is now grandstanding as a *"player"* for world peace. Can their dictator be trusted to keep the peace? I frankly doubt it. [5]Jesus predicts unless divine intervention takes place sometime in this century; humanity will destroy itself.

Iran and other nations are a continual deterrent to the peace of the Middle East nations, especially over the nation Israel. These **ancient Persians** have caused trouble in the Middle East for centuries. Just like the attack of "911"; how quickly things can change on this planet. Americans tend to forget the long road of tragic bombings and terrorist attacks innocent people have suffered from these terrorist sponsor nations for more than 40 years.

---

[4] *Luke 16:15-16*

(15) And he said unto them, Ye are they which justify yourselves before men; but God knows your hearts: for the highly esteemed among men is abomination in the sight of God.

(16) <u>The law and the prophets were until John</u>: since that time, **the kingdom of God is preached***, and every man presses into it.*

[5] *Matthew 24:22*

(22) And except those days should be shortened, there should no flesh be saved: but for the elect's sake those days shall be shortened.

You must be willing to study the history and problems humanity has created for itself to understand why we are headed toward a **New World Order** and **Armageddon**. The concept of political correctness and liberalism creates feelings of miss-trust among governments and nations. A lack of trust among our leaders grows like a cancer. Our nation cannot seem to return to common-sense thinking. We have lost our ability to be the influential leader for nations in the world. We are a nation founded upon the Judeo-Christian basics for leadership in the world; But we have allowed the same attitudes of Ancient Israel and secular ancient Rome to replace our Godly and good sense principles. We have fallen victim to political correctness and liberalism. Liberalism has compromised the very things God calls sin. Humanism is the order of the day, and everyone can make their own rules about life and personal behavior. This is by design, for God will not make anyone obey His rules of behavior. It is our *"free-moral"* agency that God allows for us to choose what and how we live. It is up to the individual to choose values to live by.

The bible reveals God's Plan for the intended destiny of humanity and this earth. God's Plan is not taught by main religious and political influences of today. It has been hijacked and replaced by deceitful theology, purposely designed to cause mankind to miss the truth of our intended destiny. Satan does not want us to realize our destiny as children of God.

God has allowed humanity to make its own mistakes for the last 6,000 years. We are near the end of that time. Humanity has the capability of destroying itself and the earth. President Trump taunting the dictator of North Korea with weapons of mass destruction. Well, it is not going to happen. The world will come close to destruction. [6] But the prophecy from Jesus says there will be divine intervention and a positive outcome for humanity and the world. The bible provides the way for surviving the end-time apocalyptic prophesies of the bible.

There are some who are already living their lives as *"first responders"* and will someday pioneer the positive side of mankind's intended destiny

---

[6] *Mat 24:21-22*
(21) For then shall be great tribulation, such as was not since the beginning of the world to this time, no, nor ever shall be.
(22) And except those days should be shortened, there should no flesh be saved: but for the elect's sake those days shall be shortened.

in the final New World Order. The opportunity for becoming a *"first responder"* in the "final" New World is available for those who choose to believe what the bible reveals.

The coming Apocalypse is only the beginning of events that will eventually fulfill mankind's intended destiny and the end of the current world order. There are many worldwide events predicted to happen before Armageddon and beyond. These events are prophesied in the bible. This is what I intend to reveal in this book.

I invite you to come along this journey of history, prophesies, and prophetic interpretation to understand the coming **New World Order**, **Armageddon**, and **The Kingdom of God**.

A Cataclysmic change of the earth is now possible in our lifetime.

The scientist genius, Carl Sagan estimated 20 years ago, that enough nuclear destructive weapons exist to destroy the world over forty times. One time is enough! He characterized the situation as follows; He said, *"Think about two enemies standing in the same room knee deep in gasoline. One man has Twenty matches; the other man has One match in his hand. They both could ignite the room full of gasoline."* The outcome of this characterization illustrates it does not matter how many nuclear weapons a country has, for it only takes one nation with one nuclear weapon to start a chain reaction that will destroy this planet.

[7]The bible does speak of a final cataclysmic event upon this earth; but it will not happen until the end-time prophetic events are all fulfilled. Long before this cataclysmic event, there will be a **New World Order**, **Armageddon**, and **The Kingdom of God** established by Jesus Christ. There will be a **thousand years of peace** and prosperity in the world.

---

[7] *2Peter 3:5-9 (5) For this they willingly are ignorant of, that by the word of God the heavens were of old, and the earth standing out of the water and in the water:*
(6) Whereby the world that then was, being overflowed with water, perished:
(7) But the heavens and the earth, which are now, by the same word are kept in store, reserved unto fire against the day of judgment and perdition of ungodly men.
(8) But, beloved, be not ignorant of this one thing, that one day is with the Lord as a thousand years, and a thousand years as one day.
(9) The Lord is not slack concerning his promise, as some men count slackness; but is longsuffering to us-ward, not willing that any should perish, but that all should come to repentance.

Many who have not had a chance at Spiritual Salvation will be allowed to make their choice for their destiny. This is good news for billions of people.

- ➢ What if I tell you there is no rapture scenario for Christians to escape a Great Tribulation?
- ➢ [9]Would it shock you to know that not everyone is called to this information at this time?
- ➢ What if I tell you that Russia or China are not going to be the Beast Power in the end times scenario?
- ➢ What if I tell you radical terrorism will become an economic problem when the coming Beast *that was, is not, and yet is*; mentioned in your bible, becomes reality?
- ➢ What if I tell you the Great false prophet of Revelation is already a position with worldwide recognition and will someday appear as the Great Peacemaker of a new world order?
- ➢ What if I tell you there will be a Third Temple built in Jerusalem by the Jews?
- ➢ What if I tell you the Jews and Catholic leaders believe they are the intended moral leaders for the world and will claim that power with the coming Beast?
- ➢ What if I tell you the Headquarters of a New World Order of religious and political influences will be in Jerusalem, Israel, not the Vatican or Mecca, Moscow, or Hong Kong?
- ➢ What if I tell you about the Holy City with Streets of Gold is going to come to this Earth for its final resting place, not somewhere in the heavens?
- ➢ What if I tell you that the conditions you enjoy in this country are someday going to degenerate into economic disaster and anarchy in the streets?

---

[8] *John 6:44 No man can come to me, except the Father which hath sent me draw him: and I will raise him up at the last day.*

[9] *(Mat 24:21) For then shall be great tribulation, such as was not since the beginning of the world to this time, no, nor ever shall be.*

(Mat 24:22) And except those days should be shortened, there should no flesh be saved: <u>but for the elect's sake those days shall be shortened</u>.

- ➢ America will compromise its founding principles and yield its power to the United States of Europe.
- ➢ The U.S. dollar **will not** be the world currency any longer; for it will be devalued to make way for the Deutschemark or Euro Dollar. We are the only country in the world 20Trillion dollars in debt to other major world powers.
- ➢ There will be a **Fourth Reich** coming as a ***new world order*** that intends to rule the world.

You would think I have lost my mind or arrived here from some other planet. Sometimes I wonder how the great writers, scholars, preachers, and interpreters of biblical prophesies arrive at their opinions from the information the Bible contains.

First, they are not giving us the complete Gospel of Jesus Christ!

Second, they do not study or research the history of who the modern nations are today before they interpret biblical prophecy.

Third, they do not study the history of nations who have tried to conquer the world masses down through history.

The churches and religions of today are not even close to preaching what Jesus told His disciples to tell the world about the coming attempt of man for world peace, the worst tribulation in the world, Armageddon, and the coming Kingdom of God. Even the splintered churches of people who know about the coming Kingdom of God are not unified and strong together as a force to preach and teach such information. Splits and splits, opinions, and fear, dissuade them.

[10]The Gospel of Jesus Christ is not about changing people's minds; it is about warning the world and preparing an *"elect people"* of *"first responders."* God calls whomsoever He will join the saints who have lived and died. The message must be heard before they can respond. The church should be preparing people to be ready to rise and rule this world under the power and direction of Jesus Christ. There is more to the Gospel than

---

10 Matthew 24:21-22
(21) For then shall be <u>great tribulation, such as was not since the beginning of the world to this time</u>, no, nor ever shall be.
(22) And except those days should be shortened, <u>there should no flesh be saved</u>: but for the elect's sake those days shall be shortened.

teaching about pagan holidays, saving souls to fill pews, accept offerings of money, church suppers, and build larger churches. **Your church will not save you when these things become a reality!**

Establish your understanding of the bible and a personal relationship with Jesus Christ before you pick a church to attend. Pay attention to who you are spending time together with spiritually.

[11]I am reporting to you what history and the bible tells us about the *"latter days"* when humanity would destroy itself with **nuclear weapons of mass destruction**; a chain reaction of smashing atoms to the point of destruction and nuclear winter worldwide that will evaporate humanity.

This book will point the identity of what ancient nations of the bible and who they are today. The information can tell us which nations will be involved in the End Time Apocalypse. It is up to you to read and decide for yourself what history and the bible can tell us who these nations will be and why the Coming Apocalypse will happen.

There is an end coming to the realm of physical human beings. The conclusion will be Apocalyptic with two distinct destinies for humanity.

Evil is a force that will require a **Spiritual army** to remove its influence in the world. Most people do not understand what the bible reveals for the final estate of humanity and the end of the world as we know it.

My interest in prophecy is driven by the question most people ask, *"how this information affects me?"* As I study the subject of prophecy in the bible, I understand how prophecy affects me; **is up to me**. Our place and position in future events will be determined by how much we commit ourselves to allowing the living Holy Spirit of God by knowing and accepting the Complete Gospel of Jesus Christ to super-charge our human spiritual awareness. We can then look to what history and the bible can tell us regarding our potential to live a positive, productive, and balanced life.

---

[11] *Hebrews 1:1-3*

(1) God, who at sundry times and in divers' manners spoke in time past unto the fathers by the prophets,

(2) Hath in these last days spoken unto us by his son, whom he hath appointed heir of all things, by whom also he made the worlds.

(3) Who being the brightness of his glory, and the express image of his person, and upholding all things by the word of his power, when he had by himself purged our sins, sat down on the right hand of the Majesty on high.

Are we living a personal life espousing the Godly principles given to us and pioneered by Jesus Christ? Does our daily life reflect the confidence to educate ourselves by spending more time with the bible than the deceit of modern-day "*progressive*" religions? The true principles for living were carried in the hearts and minds of the *true believers* for centuries as they were persecuted, martyred, or driven from country to country. We have the freedom nowadays to pursue these truths without persecution of life. Why don't we? Mentally lazy? When these events start unfolding in a few years and they are on our front porch maybe then we will dedicate some time to study these prophesies. The choice to be left in the dark is ours.

What has happened to that "Pilgrim Spirit" the caused the Pilgrims to come to America and continue Godly principles for living? Now almost four hundred years since the Pilgrims landed at Plymouth Rock, America provides the freedom for choices related to how we live our daily lives. It has also allowed any and every conceivable act by humanity; justified under the flag of 1st amendment rights and a new smorgasbord of laws to fit most any depraved lifestyle one can imagine. We are way "left" of balance in morality.

The original **Ten Commandments** no longer have priority in this country. There is a "*likeness*" of Moses overlooking the American congress as it works each day governing our society. Moses was given the most perfect "*code of ethics to live by*" yet our congress cannot even elect people who are close to commitment in their work to these TEN COMMANDMENTS. They break all of them in one way or another. Lobbyist, Bribery, and Deceit is found in our leaders of government. Millions of dollars are spent on investigating their wicked behavior. The Senators and Congressmen are a corrupted clan of lustful, greedy, politicians seeking all they can get for themselves with the power they have. We have lost the idea that freedom is obedience to the laws of God, and not the opinions or new laws created by carnal men who sit in the "*Seat of Judgment*" in our Supreme Court.

America has done exactly what God tells ancient Israel not to do. They have allowed the false religions and the "*highjacked*" Christian religion to create a world of carnal indulgences and freedoms that will bring about the prophesies of your bible before Christ returns.

The coming **Armageddon** will usher in the **Kingdom of God**. This will be the final solution for evil in the world. This book will give you a reasonable and rational understanding of conditions ahead of us and what, where, and how the end time Apocalypse will play out on the world scene.

INTRODUCTION

This is my personal understanding after years of reading bible prophesies and other books about the **End-Times**. I have put together bible prophesies telling us the history of humanity, nations, and what God says about human nature. [12]This information is coupled with the inspired prophesies of the Old Testament prophets and the final prophet, **Jesus Christ** and what He has to say.

Some people think Prophecy is a fantasy conjured up to scare the *"hell"* out of people. The bible is a scary book, if you are on the wrong side of the wrath of God. However, I do not think the subject is a fantasy for the mind. The bible is a reliable source of information documenting the past. It provides information about what is predicted, happened in academic history, and will happen in the future. Regardless of what critics want us to believe about the bible, its prophesies are accurate in fulfillment. Even the bible provides a rule for us to consider.

Jeremiah 28:9

The prophet which prophesies of peace, when the word of the prophet shall happen, then shall the prophet be known, that the LORD hath truly sent him.

Many of the prophetic dreams, visions, and close encounters of the writers have come to pass and are identified as facts of academic history. History is proof the prophetic writings have happened in academic history. The future prophesies are *"wait and see"* and can happen in this 21st century.

---

[12] *Revelation 19:10*
*(10) And I fell at his feet to worship him. And he said unto me, see thou do it not: I am thy fellow servant, and of thy brethren that have the testimony of Jesus: worship God: for the testimony of **Jesus is the spirit of prophecy.***

In these modern times humanity, can forecast the weather, stock market values, and economic trends. The forecasts are based on **historical behavior** of physical events, repeatability, and watching past and present information related to the events. This often provides a **predictable path of events** toward the outcome of final events. Biblical prophesies forecast **probable outcomes** for the coming **Armageddon** and the **Kingdom of God**!

Human nature is predictable and changes truly little unless **circumstantial influence is imposed upon its normal behavior.**

Academic history and biblical history provide a dependable *"compass"* to give us direction down the path of mankind's responses to God. This can be documented creating a reasonable amount of certainty about events predicted for our near future. This is where I have created some charts of past prophesies and historical events to illustrate the accuracy of prophecy. Many prophesies of the Old Testament have been fulfilled, such as world kingdoms, the Messiah, destruction of Temple in Jerusalem, captivity of the Jews and so forth.

In this book, you will see [13]**"Jesus is the spirit of prophecy."** In both the book of Matthew and Revelation **Jesus is predicting and warning about coming events that would happen in 70 A.D. and in the latter days of our time.**

When you read the details of background information, you will see a logical foundation created to forecast the coming New World Order and Armageddon. I believe a subject as important and controversial as an end-time scenario of world events deserves **detailed information** from academic history, origin of nations, and bible prophecy. The bible prophesies reveal motives and reasons for events leading up to the coming **Kingdom of God.**

One should not just dive into the subject by carelessly assuming your personal wisdom, assessment, and interpretation of prophetic context is accurate.

---

[13] *Hebrews 1:1-3*
(1) God, who at sundry times and in divers' manners spoke in time past unto the fathers by the prophets,
(2) Hath in these last days spoken unto us by his son, whom he hath appointed heir of all things, by whom also he made the worlds.
(3) Who being the brightness of his glory, and the express image of his person, and upholding all things by the word of his power, when he had by himself purged our sins, sat down on the right hand of the Majesty on high.

There are rules required for a **rational approach** to understanding the prophesies of the bible. When rules are applied to the writings of the prophets and compared with the fulfilled prophesies, they cause **predicted events** to come into focus and clarity. This information and a desire to know, reveals the plan of God for humanity found in bible prophecy. God can help us understand the reason for the prophesies of the bible. There are also rules that apply to the study of biblical prophecy. One basic rule is, **let the bible interpret the bible**. Much of the mysterious language reveals itself if you connect other passages of scripture in the bible to the context of a prophetic writing or vision.

Another rule is to **categorize the information; known, unknown, and speculation,** for analysis. With these rules one can come to a **rational conclusion** for what prophesies could mean for our future. However, God reserves a certain amount of information to be left to speculation.

I do see a special gift for authoring this book; it is the *latent influence* of the Holy Spirit bearing upon a humble desire to understand how events for mankind and the world will play out in the future. There is a logic revealing who some of the modern nations and leaders will be prior to the final **new world order.**

This book will contain information to understand the prophesies of the End-Time with a degree of accuracy and logic. People today pay money to *"mystics"* and *"fortune tellers"* to investigate their future. The bible has answers if they are willing to work, exert time, and study to search out the information.

You need a **background from research of ancient history.** This creates the foundational information for the revelation prophesies will reveal. This involves rules for prophetic study, coupled with historic comparisons, along with the attributes and characteristics of nations of people in history God has dealt with. Much of our academic history validates the many prophesies are already fulfilled.

It is an important process to acquire a logical understanding in the human nature of men and nations. **One must understand the *"Beast,"* described in Daniel and Revelation, is a world dominating government of men influenced by a Religious System that justifies the power of the Beast forcing the people of the world under domination of the *"beast power."***

Since the Tower of Babel event, the **Babylonian Mystery Religious** system has corrupted the true destiny of humanity. All the major wars down through time have been attempts to rule the world by some dictatorial despot lusting for power. Religion has been one of the tools to maintain control of the human mind.

The world scene is moving closer to what Jesus said to watch for in world events, and I feel an unction from God to present what the Holy Spirit impressed upon my years of research and study about prophesy.

There is a cry for information other than *"establishment"* information in government politics and religious teachings in our country today; so, what I am sharing in this book is what I believe will prepare us to understand there is a coming of the **Kingdom of God** to this earth.

This book is different than the pre-digested information of early Century doctrines and beliefs churches promote about the end-time prophesies. These subjects about historic **proclivities** and **prophesies** are rarely taught or discussed in churches or Sunday school lessons. Prophesies are rarely preached from the pulpits in the mainstream churches. A new world government is the goal of humanity and its search for world peace. The bible reveals the failure of governments of men in the writings of the prophets and **Jesus Christ's full gospel to humanity.** Christ's complete gospel includes God's plan for mankind's true destiny for world peace, eternal salvation, peace, and prosperity.

We need a detailed study of the coming changes in world order and who the main players could be. The Book of Revelation will be referenced. [14]It is the final prophesy from Jesus Christ to humanity. It will reveal the *"keys"* to unlocking the mysterious metaphors of prophesy. It will inform you of heavenly scenes that exist today and heavenly events and signs for the future. I will break down the information of each chapter, pulling pieces of the puzzle out of them and putting them in a "timeline" order of events.

There is a final summary of the events to explore beyond Armageddon. It will outline the future **New World Order of Jesus Christ** for humanity and the many events you never hear about in your churches. It will shock you to see the true plan of God compared to what most religions teach about your final destiny as a human being.

---

14   **Romans 1:18** For the wrath of God is revealed from heaven against all ungodliness and unrighteousness of men, who hold the truth in unrighteousness;

I will be using the KJV for all scripture references. I will use the Strong's concordance for better contextual definition of the English words used, for clarity and accuracy of the prophet's writings. The historical information comes from my notes over 40 years of interest in academic and biblical history. I want to understand how the near future will play out on the world scene. This is a story that is more than just "*doom and gloom.*" There is a world of great peace and prosperity for humanity after these events triggered by mankind are past.

Many of the books written on prophecy contain a fair amount of biblical support; but I question the writers to have exposed themselves to enough historical information, biblical teachings, prayer, and honesty to interpret the bible prophesies. It is imperative to understand true history and recognize the trends of peoples and religions. Before an opinion of who the players will be in the end-time scenario of prophesies can be made, foundational information must be established. One must get the background information organized from the time of these prophesies to the present-day information. Timeline is imperative in resolving biblical prophetic writings. Following the history of nations, leaders, and political agendas through the history of humanity and nations of powerful people is necessary, especially for a clear assessment of the reasons for a new order. There is a lot of background and foundational information to cover to accurately assess predicted events leading up to the **new world order created by men of power**. Many other scriptures from the bible must be considered and fit into a time-line revelation of the end-time scenario of information.

Religion is a major player in the deceit and false information since the Roman Empire "*hijacked*" the true Gospel from Jesus Christ shortly after the murder of the Apostles. The Roman Catholic Empire of ancient times is, to this very day, influencing the people of the world with the traditions of the ancient **Babylonian Mystery Religion.**

[15]The people are not the problem; it is the system and leadership of the Churches. This is keeping the false belief sustained.

---

15   ***Hebrews 1:1-2*** *God, who at sundry times and in different manners spoken <u>in time past unto the fathers by the prophets</u>, (2) Has <u>in these last days spoken unto us by his Son</u>, whom he hath appointed **heir of all things, by whom also he made the worlds.*** ***Daniel*** *2:44 (44) And in the days of these kings shall the God of heaven set up a kingdom, which shall never be destroyed: and the kingdom shall not be left to other people, but it shall break in pieces and consume all these kingdoms, and it shall stand for ever.*

The new world order by humanity is the final establishment of the **Religious System** started by the ancient **Babylonians.** It is created just after the flood of Noah's time. It is resurrected just a few years after Jesus and the Apostles are murdered and continues to present day. The prophesies concerning the near future tell us what conditions to look for prior to the **Second Coming of Christ.** These events can only happen in this end time of mankind's technological power and knowledge. We are living in times of worldwide communication; at the click of a mouse humanity can launch nuclear weapons of mass destruction.

Centuries have come and gone while this prophetic knowledge has been available in your Bible. Some of the information can only make sense as we progress to the end times of technology. We are close to the time when the fulfillment of these prophesies is possible.

The conditions in the world are unstable and could go in the direction of these prophetic predictions in our lifetime.

[16]We must never forget that **Jesus is the last and greatest Prophet.** Jesus tells us through John's recorded Revelation what to look for and expect. All our hopes and understanding of the future must be founded upon His love and concern for humanity. If we put our trust in the Father, Jesus, and Holy Spirit we can surely get a logical glimpse of what to expect in the **coming Kingdom of God.**

There is a new world order coming by the hand of humanity, but it will not last! The final New World Order **will not** be administrated by the

---

16   *Revelation 19:11-16*

(11) And I saw heaven opened and behold a white horse; and he that sat upon him was called Faithful and True, and in righteousness he doth judge and make war.

(12) His eyes were as a flame of fire, and on his head were many crowns; and he had a name written, that no man knew, but he himself.

(13) And he was clothed with a vesture dipped in blood: and his name is called The Word of God.

(14) And the armies which were in heaven followed him upon white horses, clothed in fine linen, white and clean.

(15) And out of his mouth goes a sharp sword, that with it he should smite the nations: and he shall rule them with a rod of iron: and he treads the winepress of the fierceness and wrath of Almighty God.

(16) And he hath on his vesture and on his thigh a name written, KING OF KINGS, AND LORD OF LORDS.

governments of men! [17]Jesus is coming back as the King of Kings and Lord of Lord's in what your bible reveals is the establishment of the **KINGDOM OF GOD upon this earth!** When He comes, will you be ready?

---

[17] Rev 13:12-15

(12) And he exercises all the power of the first beast before him and causes the earth and them which dwell therein to worship the first beast, whose deadly wound was healed.

(13) And he doeth great wonders, so that he makes fire come down from heaven on the earth in the sight of men,

(14) And deceives them that dwell on the earth by the means of those miracles which he had power to do in the sight of the beast; saying to them that dwell on the earth, that they should make an image to the beast, which had the wound by a sword, and did live.

(15) And he had power to give life unto the image of the beast, that the image of the beast should both speak, and cause that as many as would not worship the image of the beast should be killed.

Matthew 24:24

(24) For there shall arise false Christs, and false prophets, and shall shew great signs and wonders; insomuch that, if it were possible, they shall deceive the very elect.

PERSONAL FROM THE AUTHOR

When you read this book, consider the information with biblical proof texts provided, I believe you will be blessed with an understanding of the divine prophetic writings God inspires the Prophets to tell us to expect before the "Second Coming of Christ." These events have been prophesied since the days of Old Testament prophets, especially Daniel. It will give insight for knowing what to expect in the future. In the light of the bible, some academic historical events predicted are demonstrated to have already been fulfilled. Most people do not understand the bible is about World Government, the governments of men and the coming government of God to this earth.

SPECULATION

Let us speculate for a minute. Who will be the false prophet in the end-time scenario? The candidate is the **Pope of Rome**. *He is the one who claims to be the Vicar of Christ all down through history. The recent Pope has been only the fourth to ever visit the Holy City of Jerusalem where the final scenario will play out. The Jewish leadership rolled out the "red carpet" for him during his historic visit. What if they were to believe he is the Messiah?* [18]*Especially since the bible says he will demonstrate signs of great power and wonder. What if the Pope could negotiate a peace agreement between Israel and Palestine? The Jews would see him as the Messiah they believe has not come yet. They would offer him the new temple in Jerusalem they have built. This "false prophet" would then establish a "world order" based on peace and prosperity for all nations who willingly participate in his "new world order." The United States of Europe*

---

[18] Matthew 3:1-3
   (1) In those days came John the Baptist, preaching in the wilderness of Judaea,
   (2) And saying, Repent ye: for the kingdom of heaven is at hand.
   (3) For this is her that was spoken of by the prophet Esaias, saying, the voice of one crying in the wilderness, prepare ye the way of the Lord, make his paths straight.

led by a German Military force would finance and be the administrator of world trade. The United States of America would have to join the European Common Market to survive because of its economic demise and the devalue of the dollar as a world currency. Jerusalem would become the center of world religious power and economic prosperity. A pseudo world peace would be created with all nations cooperating with the "beast and false prophet" as their leaders. This could last at least the 3.5 years the bible prophesies. World trade and ecumenical understanding between nations and religions would beget a peaceful trade and security for all nation participating.

[19]Where is the voice "crying in the wilderness" for people to change their complacent ways, leave their comfort zones, and stand up to call out the sins of the churches and the world? [20]Where is the "watchman" warning Christians and the world about where they are headed if this current trend in thinking does not stop? The church age established by Christ is supposed to be fulfilling these two aspects of what God wants the people of the world to know. This message is not what a football stadium full of Christians are hearing. If it were preached, the stadium would not be full, because most people are too comfortable with life. They are made to feel good about their life by what these less than John the Baptist or Elijah quality preachers are teaching.

The current issues of our day will mean something more to you as they are starting to head the nations down a path of the prophesied events in our not-too-distant future. These events will usher in a **new world order** by the enforcement of man's style of government.

---

[19] Ezekiel 33:1-5
(1) Again, the word of the LORD came unto me, saying,
(2) Son of man, speak to the children of thy people, and say unto them, When I bring the sword upon a land, if the people of the land take a man of their coasts, and set him for their watchman:
(3) If when he sees the sword come upon the land, he blows the trumpet, and warn the people.
(4) Then whosoever hears the trumpet, and taketh not warning; if the sword come, and take him away, his blood shall be upon his own head.
(5) He heard the trumpet and took not warning; his blood shall be upon him. But he that taketh warning shall deliver his soul.

[20] Amos 3:7
(7) Surely the Lord GOD will do nothing, but he reveals his secret unto his servants the prophets.

*I am providing a large amount of foundational background information to lead you in a comprehensive and chronological view of the broad movements of God revealed in these prophesies! Prophesies reveal the **Plan of God for mankind's ultimate destiny.***

In my first book, **Why You Were Born***, I begin at the very genesis of mankind's appearance on earth and how God collaborated with individuals and later begins to work with nations. This book presents details of the physical and spiritual applications of God's Plan for humanity. A firm background of information is a priority for investigation and understanding to any complete* **eschatological system** *that defines our destiny. This book will demonstrate the details of how the ultimate destiny of humanity will play out.*

A framework of tremendous revelations will appear concerning the "times of the Gentiles" and the program for Israel to learn the aspects of God's redemption plan for humanity. You will discover there are many prophetic writings from the Old Testament, but **only one private teaching** *and* **one visionary book** *in the New Testament that connects the answers. The teaching is the Mount Olivet Prophecy from Jesus to His disciples; the book is the Apocalypse or Revelation of Jesus Christ to John the apostle. These prophesies are visionary and symbolic in nature.*

The fact that a biblical book is **apocalyptic** *does not render its content obscure or uncertain. Apocalyptic revelation is a genuine form of divine communication which is recognized by most all conservative scholars and theologians regarding the ultimate destiny of humanity. [21]God wants you to know these things. But you must believe and be willing to spend some time reading about coming events. I hope this book will shed some light on some of it.*

The interpretation of apocalyptic writings requires close attention to **eschatology of timelines** *as they apply to its revelation. Therefore, a scriptural history from the very beginning of the bible will prove its validation to the plan of God in many of the later prophesies when applied to a timeline.*

In the light of world conditions today it is possible to understand with a reasonable amount of certainty many events that will precede the second coming of Christ. For Christians living in the age of grace today, this fundamental background information will shed a broad light upon these prophetic predictions for the end-times ahead of us.

---

[21]   *Romans 3:23 For all have sinned, and come short of the glory of God;*

I urge my readers to take the time to absorb this foundational information for prophetic interpretation and the historical past for information that must be considered. History is not an easy subject to present and keep people interested in future events. However, it is necessary work; coupled with patience, to understand end-time prophesies with confidence and peaceful certainty.

Ancient history reveals two brothers who are completely different in their approach to life. From the post-flood era of Noah, their jealousy and differences crop up in their generations that follow. This pattern of behavior culminates in the battle of Armageddon. [22]*The Apostle Paul said that we all have faults that we must eventually overcome. When certain genetic proclivities are not overcome by the Holy Spirit, carnal human nature operates unchecked and can lead to the end time Armageddon.*

You will acquire a peaceful certainty in God's great overall plan for mankind including your opportunity to live forever, a life far greater than we can imagine by the end of this book!

- *There is a New World Order coming. A beast power and a false prophet will administer it.*
- *Armageddon will follow the New World Order by humanity.*
- *Armageddon will end with* **the coming of Jesus Christ to this earth to establish His New World Order!**

It is a long road of slow progression and catastrophic events resulting in a near destruction of humanity and the earth as we know it. It will be "sad news" followed by "good news" before true peace can come to this world. Your bible predicts it, and God will see that it is fulfilled. It is a story that mainstream religions do not preach and teach.

There will be a group of "first-responders" or as the bible teaches, "first-fruits" that will rule the world under the direction of Jesus Christ! You can be a part of **God's New World Order** *if you choose to let go of predigested false doctrines and teachings about the true destiny for humanity. You can prepare yourself with a personal relationship with God the Father and Jesus your savior!*

---

[22] **Hebrews 1:1-2 KJV**

(1) God, who at sundry times and in different manners spoke in time past unto the fathers by the prophets,
(2) Hath <u>in these last days spoken unto us by his son</u>, whom he hath appointed heir of all things, by whom also he made the worlds.

I challenge you to study the information from this book with your bible and see what God allows you to see and understand when you truly surrender pre-conceived belief in Jesus and see what the bible truly reveals for our future!

Charles L. Pope

UPDATE: As this book was being finished the news has just said that the Democrats are setting the stage to impeach President Trump. This could be another step toward the New World Order that is coming. The greatest country since WWII is becoming divided, in extreme debt, and complete disarray in the eyes of the world. Divide and conquer is the devil's game. A house divided will not stand for long. If the President is impeached, what will the effect be on this nation? Could this be the beginning of the downfall of America? Will the countries we owe call for their debts? If so, it could bankrupt America. We are living in the end time of prophetic events. We are on the edge of many biblical prophesies beginning to become known and reality.

Things are lining up quickly for a coming New World Order to be promoted. Will America survive this order of events? It is a wait and see proposition for Christians. Jesus said, "Watch for you know not what time your savior comes." As you will see at the end of this book,

"EVEN SO, COME LORD JESUS"

CHAPTER ONE
Foundational Background Information

"It is essential to create a foundation of information for understanding prophecy. Prophecy is certainly of no private interpretation, so says scripture. However, I believe a person can study prophesies and come to a reasonable opinion for an event that is prophesied. I believe with substantial information and logic; an interpretation is possible without bias. It is certainly possible when one believes the Holy Spirit of God prompts our logical process for seeking answers."

THE ACCURACY OF PROPHECY

Much of the bible is prophecy. In the Old Testament are many references to events prophesied and fulfilled. An example are the many prophesies foretelling the birth of the Savior or Messiah.

[23]The last prophet was Jesus Christ and there has not been another after Him.

There are at least four main themes of prophecy in the Old Testament.
- ➢ Prophesies concerning the coming of the Messiah.
- ➢ Prophesies concerning the Kingdoms or world governments of humanity.
- ➢ Prophesies concerning Armageddon and the second coming of Jesus Christ.
- ➢ The establishment of the Kingdom of God on Earth.

Christians understand faith and hope come by believing in Jesus Christ. We can have peace of mind in the word of God and the prophesies. Through the power of the Holy Spirit witnessing with our spirit, we acquire knowledge for our peace of mind. The promise of the Holy Spirit's influence, upon our minds, is one of the great promises enabling us to understand the deep things from God. Christians are an example of divine nature within us opposing evil and unethical behavior in our personal life.

Acquiring knowledge strengthens faith, temperance, patience, charity, and kindness toward our fellowman. Because of our belief in God, we understand prophesies with a future and look forward to our place in a coming Kingdom.

---

[23] *2Peter 1:16-21*

(16) For we have not followed cunningly devised fables when we made known unto you the power and coming of our Lord Jesus Christ but were eyewitnesses of his majesty.

(17) For he received from God the Father honor and glory, when there came such a voice to him from the excellent glory, this is my beloved Son, in whom I am well pleased.

(18) And this voice which came from heaven we heard when we were with him in the holy mount.

(19) We have also a surer word of prophecy; whereunto ye do well that ye take heed, as unto a light that shines in a dark place, until the day dawn, and the day star arise in your hearts:

(20) Knowing this first, that no prophecy of the scripture is of any private interpretation.

(21) For the prophecy came not in old time by the will of man: but holy men of God spoke as they were moved by the Holy Spirit.

God wants us to be established by truth not allowing ourselves to be deceived.

Therefore, personal bible study must be a priority. Each time you read your bible; it is time with our God and Savior. Read the writings of the prophets and know them like your friends. The Holy Spirit will help you witness with them. It is conversation with God, for God inspired what they wrote. [24]We also have the witness of the apostles. about the plan of God.

Peter is there on the mount hearing the voice of God. Peter hears the voice from heaven, the sure word of prophecy concerning the birth of Christ written centuries before Christ was born. Peter finds himself standing there with Jesus. Peter says we should study and pay attention to prophesies, because they are a light shining into the darkness of curiosity until our mind understands what the future holds for us.

There has always been a conflict between good and evil. Since the garden of Eden, Satan has been the deceiver and destroyer of humanity. History repeats itself with wars and wars of religious and political nature. A steady flow of interrupted peace and war. Is there any time you can think of that a conflict is not occurring somewhere in the world?

BACKGROUND KNOWLEDGE

Complete background knowledge for the purpose of interpreting biblical prophesies requires a combination of biblical, academic history, and modern science. Much of the early history from the writings of Moses creates a lot of "blanks" in the post-flood history of humanity. These "blanks" can be filled in by comparing the bible with ancient academic records. The Akkadian Epic is one such document that is helpful. It is an academic record of certain ethnic groups of people and their kings who walked the earth after the flood.

It is also necessary to create a background of knowledge from the books of the bible. The book of Daniel is one of these books. The writing of Daniel is an apocalyptic book. Apocalyptic, because of the character of the

---

[24] *Isaiah 36:1*

(1) Now it came to pass in the fourteenth year of king Hezekiah, that **Sennacherib king of Assyria** *came up against all the defensed cities of Judah, and took them.*

supernatural visions. These are intimated by the Greek word, *Apokalypsis*, meaning an unveiling of truth.

The book of Daniel is the most comprehensive prophetic revelation from the **Old Testament.** It reveals a brief view of world history, from the time of Babylon until the second coming of Christ. Daniel provides an overall *"key"* to interpretation of prophecy. Its prophesies are connected to the book of Revelation in the **New Testament**. Daniel's contribution to **eschatology** is evident by his theme containing history. Daniel's writings provide the only Old Testament narrative outlining the Plan of God for the salvation of humanity. It predicts Christ's first coming and his second coming. This is called the 70 Weeks Prophecy.

The Mount of Olives discourse Christ delivers to His disciples the last week of His life on earth in 30 A.D. is also foundational information to many of the writings in the book of Revelation. (Revelation is written by the Apostle John in about 97 A.D.)

These scriptures, from your bible reveal the events leading up to and beyond Armageddon. They are the foundation for this book.

- The book of Daniel
- Matthew 24:1-28
- I Corinthians 15:50-58
- I Thessalonians 4:13-18
- I Thessalonians 4:1-11
- II Thessalonians 1:7-12
- II Thessalonians 2:1-10
- II Peter 1:16-21
- II Peter 2:1-22
- II Peter 3:1-13
- I John 2:18-27
- I John 4:1-3
- Jude 1:1-23
- The book of Revelation

These are just a few of the passages that are in the bible. One third of the bible is about prophecy. Isiah, Jeremiah, and Ezekiel are full of end—time information.

The path to Armageddon is because of the failures of the kingdoms of men. I reveal some of this journey in my first book, **Why You Were Born**. In that book, I explore the first government created by Nimrod. This conquest to rule people begins at the Tower of Babel. Humanity is influenced and eventually ruled by people of power and popularity. In ancient times, the governing of people becomes a mixture of *religious* and *circumstantial* need. Government is needed because of the world-wide flood and rebuilding the population of humanity.

Out of this post-flood world were two brothers born to Shem, one of Noah's sons. Their names are **Assur** and **Araxphad**. The main thing I want you to remember about these two brothers is how opposite their approach to life was.

ASSUR AND ARAXPHAD

"Who Are They?"

These are the twin sons of **Shem**. Shem is the second born son of Noah. The bible hints to this fact of twin brothers in the scriptures born to Shem. Genesis 10.22 lists five sons, Elam, Assur, Araxphad, Lud and Aram. Now in Genesis 11:10 it says, "Araxphad was born two years after the flood." In other words, Elam was born the first year after the flood and his two brothers a year later. It is impossible to have three births in two years unless twins are born the second year. I will first outline the story of Assur and his generations down through history and how they are connected to recent and future history regarding world domination.

ASSUR

Many historians believe there is ample proof that **Assur** may well have been **Sargon the Great** of academic history. Assur could have changed his name to Sargon out of rebellion because Shem rejected him due to his barbaric behavior. (speculation) He was the first warlord of the Assyrian records and was regarded as the most mighty and famous of all Assyrian kings. Sargon is the Akkadian equivalent of the priest Melchizedek, meaning "True King." He was a strong leader and built many cities. He was an authoritarian with centralized government. From this man came the longest line of conquerors of any nation before Rome. Sad to say he was a racist. He was determined to make his people the *"super race"* in Babylon. (Ever heard this idea before?) He believed in segregation. Next are some points that Assur is Sargon.

- Sargon lived during the same time as Assur.
- Assur and Sargon possessed the same characteristics, militaristic, despotic, and cruel.
- Many of the Assyrian Kings (descendants of Assur) were named after Sargon.
- Sargon despised other races.
- The Jewish historian Josephus says Assur's name means 'strong' and 'powerful.' It should be noted that in front of an ancient temple to Assur is dis-played swastika on limestone.
- Assur could have changed his name to Sargon because his father Shem rejected his behavior.

The Jewish historian Josephus says that **Assur** built and lived at the city of Nineveh and called his subjects, **Assyrians**. *(It should be noted that God uses the Ancient Assyrian people to punish His chosen people, Israel many times in the bible)* Josephus says they became the most fortunate cities among others because of their conquests. They were pagans and their supreme god was Asshur. Assyrian kings hunted Lions. Lions became an important symbol of the Assyrian Empire. Another prominent symbol was the Eagle.

Sargon was highly praised and looked upon as a god. Therefore, he was the principal god of the Assyrian people. The fact that Sargon was a racist is evident by his defeat and incarceration of Lugalzzaggisi (Nimrod) son of Cush. (Nimrod was half black.) Sargon's empire came from the North upon them like a whirlwind (*blitzkrieg-type*). Sargon was set on making his people the *"master race"* in Babylon. This is because the founders of Babylon were dark Hamites. The Assyrian armies came to be called the Prussians of the Ancient world. They were fully militarized and enormously powerful. (Sounds a lot like Germany of WWII.) *(Emphasis mine)*

Following Sargon a few of very terrible and strong kings from the linage of Assur.

- Tiglath-Pileser I
- Sargon II
- [25][26]Sennacherib
- Esarhaddon
- Assurbanipal
- Shalmaneser I

The Assyrian Empire experienced at least 70 years of peace as they enforced their will upon any invading barbaric tribes. They became the guardians to safeguard the civilized world.

Now not all Assyrians are descended from Assur. They had to incorporate foreign conquered forces to help sustain their power in the vast region. This allowed some mixing of tribes over time.

MILITARY CHARACTERISTICS

Assyria became a great commercial and military power in the world. They became a nation that perfected "*despotism.*" They are famous for their cruelty and merciless actions against their captors. It has been said that there has not existed a power so purely destructive, so **devoid** of a desire to make any substantial contribution to the welfare of humanity,

---

[25] *2Kings 19:16-17*

(16) LORD, bow down thine ear, and hear: open, LORD, thine eyes, and see: **and hear the words of Sennacherib,** *which hath sent him to reproach the living God. (17) Of a truth, LORD, the kings of Assyria have destroyed the nations and their lands,*

[26] *2Kings 18:31-32*

*(31) Hearken not to Hezekiah***: for thus saith the king of Assyria,** *Make an agreement with me by a present, and come out to me, and then eat ye every man of his own vine, and every one of his fig tree, and drink ye every one the waters of his cistern: (32) Until I come and take you away to a land like your own land, a land of corn and wine, a land of bread and vineyards, a land of oil olive and of honey, that ye may live, and not die: and* **hearken not unto Hezekiah***, when he persuades you, saying, The LORD will deliver us.*

as **Assyria**. Even their conquered peoples lived in fear and terror of the Assyrian Secret Service. (*Remind you of SS Gestapo?*) Their agents were taught to purposely be cruel and savage to their conquered people. They would sever ears, fingers, lower lips, and pour hot asphalt onto their faces. They burned whole towns and skinned the rulers alive or impaled them. They seemed dedicated to spreading bloodshed, ruin, and indiscriminate slaughter wherever they were. It is said that from the time of Shalmaneser on they called themselves "*Kings of the World.*" (*Can you think of similar actions toward a race of people 75 years ago by a nation?*)

Assyrians, the descendants of Assur, eventually become known as Germans.

Many historians say that **Tiglath-Pileser 1**, is the ancient form and **character of Hitler.** This Assyrian King wrote, *"I flayed chief men of the city of the rebels and covered the walls with their skins. Some I buried alive in the bricks of the walls as they were being built."*

I could share more horror stories from historical records, but you get the point. The Assyrians had such a great belief in themselves and their pagan god Asshur, they convinced themselves they were on a "*divine mission."* (*This is remarkably similar thinking to the Reich Concept*)

They viewed themselves as the **superior race** and exploited their captives as a source of cheap human material for forced labor. (*Not unlike what was done to the Jews in WWII*)

[27]Not only did they destroy people, they ravaged the lands also. They even dug up the trees and carried them away. They cut down all large trees resulting in industry being destroyed and an entire economy shattered.

---

[27]   *Ezekiel 37:24-26*

(24) And David my servant shall be king over them; and they all shall have one shepherd: they shall also walk in my judgments, and observe my statutes, and do them.

(25) And they shall dwell in the land that I have given unto Jacob my servant, wherein your fathers have dwelt; and they shall dwell therein, even they, and their children, and their children's children for ever: and my servant David shall be their prince for ever.

(26) Moreover I will make a covenant of peace with them; it shall be an everlasting covenant with them: and I will place them, and multiply them, and will set my sanctuary in the midst of them for evermore.

[28]The bible confirms the Assyrians even used propaganda against their enemies taunting them to surrender.

ASSYRIAN LEGACY

The fearsome Assyrians were forced to leave their "*fatherland*," The Scythians united with the Medes and destroyed the cruel Assyrian Empire. This happened around **612 B.C.** The Assyrians were captives of the **Scythians**. The Scythians were a collection of many tribes such as Elamites and Sarmatian hordes. As these tribes absorbed the Assyrian people, there was a tendency to confuse them with the Scythians. This is when the Romans introduced the name, 'German' and the name Scythian was dropped for the name **Germans.**

In other words, the nation within the collection of nations called *Scythians* became known as Germans. The combination of all these tribes reflects the artforms and psychology of Babylonia or Assyria. The Assyrian barbarian culture had disappeared from about 612 B.C. However, Archeologist have proven they became known under other tribal names such as Nordic-Kelts. As early as the 3rd century B.C. there were certain races called **'German'**. They settled north of the Alps. Most older *dictionaries* state, "*The Germans were a branch of the great Indo-Germanic race, along with the Celts, migrated into Europe from the Caucasus and the countries around the Black and Caspian Seas.*"

We know nothing of the Germans until they suddenly appear about **100 B.C.** At that time, they were aggressive enemies of the **Romans**.

The famous historian Jerome wrote, "*Savage tribes in countless numbers have overrun all parts of Gaul. The whole country between the Rhine and the Ocean, has been laid waste by hordes of Quadi Vandals, Sarmatians, Alans, Gepids, Herules, Saxons, Burgundians, and others. Assur has joined with them, and the city has been destroyed.*"

---

[28] ***Exodus 19:5-6***

(5) Now therefore, if ye will obey my voice indeed, and keep my covenant, then ***ye shall be a peculiar treasure unto me above all people****: for all the earth is mine: (6) And* ***ye shall be unto me a kingdom of priests, and an holy nation****. These are the words which thou shalt speak unto the children of Israel.*

The Assyrians reached Central Europe and settled in beautiful **Germany**; their reputation as fearless warriors spread with them. For now, let us leave the Assyrian legacy at 612 B.C. and explore Assur's twin brother **Araxphad.**

ARAXPHAD

As I stated earlier, **Assur** and **Araxphad** were twin sons of Shem, son of Noah. The name Shem means, *"men of name"* or *"distinction"*- *"the titled or noble race."* Both these brothers as we will see are ancestors of great people and talented. Araxphad must have displayed these qualities consistently; for God eventually covenants with his descendants, Abraham, Isaac, and Jacob. *(Jacob later named Israel, having 12 sons known as the 12 tribes of Israel)*

As we explored Assur's descendants, we saw they were great warriors and Assyrian kings up until 100 B. C. when they become known as Scythians or Germans as named by the Romans. Now let us follow the descendants of Araxphad. Often spelled Arpachshad, his linage traces to Abram or later called Abraham, of the bible.

Araxphad is part of a line that extends all the way back to Seth, the son of Adam and Eve. Down through history these have been the descendants of people God chose to covenant with to educate the world about the great human destiny for mankind. As I wrote in my first book, **Why You Were Born,** God worked with just a handful of people, one on one, before Moses and the Israelites. It should be noted that God chose and called Israelites to physical salvation and blessings. During that time, there were some among them who were special with the Spirit of God within them. Later in history this *"spiritual dimension"* grew when Jesus died and sent the Holy Spirit power back to mankind for those who would believe. As Jesus told the Samaritan woman at Jacob's well, *"God's church is Spiritual."* We who believe are part of the Spiritual Israelites today.

It is important to understand that God chose Israel for His people to lead the world in the intended way of life. [29]They have the religious supremacy and will be restored in the future as leaders in the Kingdom of God under King David.

[30]Back in ancient times, God was using a nation which was small, yet with excellent capacities, to confound the other nations. They possessed attributes inherited from **Araxphad,** their forefather, giving them the ability to rule, be inventive and law abiding more than other peoples of the earth. Yes, the linage of Araxphad goes down to Abraham, Isaac, and Jacob. Ancient Israel was to function as God's representatives on earth.

The original spelling is a corruption of "Khasdim" or "Chaldeans." The original Chaldeans descend from Araxphad. It becomes obvious that when God covenanted with Abram, he chose a righteous line through which He would bring truth and His way to the rest of the world. Many historians mistakenly say Abraham was a Semite. Nothing is further from truth. Abraham was from the land of [31]*Ur of the Chaldees.* This was 400 miles North of Babylon on the other side of the Euphrates River. Abraham was Chaldean.

Most of the history of Araxphad's descendants can be picked out and followed in the Old Testament scriptures. The story can be traced from Abraham, through whom God established a single family, which He would choose for leadership for other nations of the world. [32]The bible states that

---

[29] *Genesis 11:31* And Terah took *Abram his son*, and Lot the son of Haran his son's son, and Sarai his daughter in law, his son Abram's wife; and they went *forth with them from Ur of the Chaldees*, to go into the land of Canaan; and they came unto Haran, and dwelt there.

Genesis 15:7 And he said unto him*, I am the LORD that brought thee out of Ur of the Chaldees*, to give thee this land to inherit it.

[30] *Romans 4:13* For the promise, that *he should be the heir of the world*, was not to Abraham, or to his seed, through the law, but *through the righteousness of faith*.

[31] *Colossians 2:16-17*
(16) Let no man therefore judge you in meat, or in drink, or <u>in respect of an holyday</u>, or of the new moon, or of the sabbath days:
(17) Which <u>are a shadow of things to come</u>; but the body is of Christ.

[32] *Genesis 49:3-4 Reuben, thou art my firstborn, my might, and the beginning of my strength, the excellency of dignity, and the excellency of power: (4) Unstable as water, thou shalt not excel; because thou went up to thy father's bed; then defiles thou it: he went up to my couch.*

Abraham and his physical and spiritual descendants will inherit the world someday. The history of Araxphad is found with the people of the bible. This is because the bible is God's guide for the mistakes of mankind, a redemption plan, and a better life that can be eternal. *(Emphasis mine)*

I will take the time to show who the nations are today that were once called the 12 tribes of Israel. You may have heard of the lost 10 tribes of Israel; well, they are not lost! Historians do not recognize the bible as a source of valid information and have missed the prophecy about the 12 tribes of Israel and their blessings extended to the latter-days. The bible even predicted that 10 of the tribes would be scattered to other nations.

Therefore, it is important to educate ourselves about the origins of nations from ancient to modern times. Because Israel is the nation chosen by God to be the righteous influence upon the pagan nations, it is important to know who their legacy is today. The destiny of the Israelite nation is promised in a blessing over the original 12 tribes **by Israel himself**. The plan of God for mankind's salvation is memorialized through physical, religious, appointed festivals that foreshadow the actual events. It was for ancient Israel's physical salvation and a *"footprint"* for the *"church age"* Jesus started. Jesus made Spiritual Salvation possible for all who will choose it. [33]God commands these rituals, for ancient Israel, to provide a spiritual meaning that would be fulfilled in the future.

Aside from the plan, it is important to understand the origin of nations and who they are today. History bears out that Israelites have been scattered all over the world as is prophesied because of their stubborn rebellion toward the very God who chose them to be His people of representation to the rest of the nations.

The Blessings bestowed upon 12 Tribes of Israel

Over 500 years later God bestows a *"prophetic blessing"* upon **the sons of Jacob (Israel)** concerning their future legacy as nations of His people.

---

[33] ***Genesis 49:5-7** Simeon and Levi are brethren; instruments of cruelty are in their habitations. (6) O my soul, come not thou into their secret; unto their assembly, mine honor, be not thou united: for in their anger, they slew a man, and in their self-will, they dig down a wall. (7) Cursed be their anger, for it was fierce; and their wrath, for it was cruel: I will divide them in Jacob and scatter them in Israel.*

This a prophecy to guide us where these 12 nations from Israel ended up in the world after their captivity and dispersion many times down through history.

As I said earlier, nations and peoples carry certain proclivities and characteristics that are clues to their original ethnic race. True, all the peoples of today are mixes of all the different tribes and peoples of history; but there are common traits that are specific of the Israelite culture that can be identifies from these prophetic blessings.

The *"Guide to Identity"* is found in **Genesis 49** and **Deuteronomy 33** of the bible. Using these two main scriptures as guides, we can rightly interpret obscure historical evidence of these modern nations not clarified by academic history books!

THE DIFFERENCE BETWEEN ISRAEL AND ISRAEL

There is confusion that seems to exist about the modern-day nation of Israel and the legacy of ancient Israel as a 12-tribe nation that has been scattered all over the world!

Modern day Israel is a tiny nation that is formed in 1948 because of the unsettled peoples called *"Jews"* who are without a country. The post-war nations allowed them to settle in what is now called Israel. The United Nations accepts their petition to become the nation or state of Israel.

When the language of the bible in prophecies for the **"*LATTER DAYS*"** is speaking of **ISRAEL**, it is referring to a multitude of **EUOPEAN nations** and the **nation of ENGLAND and AMERICA.**

The following information will support this statement. All nations today are a mixed people from all the nations of the past world. However, some specific nations still possess the national blessings bestowed on future nations of Israel. The question has often been expressed; "where America are, Russia, China, Germany, Spain, France, Sweden, Belgium, and many other nations mentioned in the bible?"

Egypt, Ethiopia, Jordan, and many others are, why not these other nations? Hopefully, the following information will help answer this question.

The next few pages of facts may seem strange, but they are what is missing from all history books about nations! Understanding the descendants of the *"lost 10 tribes of Israel"* are not lost but *overlooked* because of historical prejudice! When you make the connection of these prophetic blessings with modern day nations of **Europe**, **England**, and **America** it opens the meaning of *"latter days"* prophesies. As you read the information you will see that England and America are descendants of Joseph! Special nations God raised up in the latter days to put down the attempt at World domination in WWI and WWII.

PERPETUAL BLESSINGS AND CHARACTERISTICS IDENTIFY NATIONS

Genesis 49:1-2 And Jacob called unto his sons, and said, gather yourselves together, that I may tell you that which shall befall you in the last days. (2) Gather yourselves together, and hear, ye sons of Jacob; and hearken unto Israel your father.

Notice that the blessings are to be perpetual to the "last days."

[34]**RUBEN** is recognized as modern day **FRANCE**. Southern France, settled by the descendants of Javan (ancient Greeks), is Gentile. A democratic country, which is unstable, yet sets the styles for the world, has the form of real excellency, and has the same sexual proclivities as Ruben.

We are all familiar with the phrase, *"finding romance in Paris, the city of love."* Just this year they demonstrated how they have their priorities wrong with the unpreparedness for the prevention of a tragic massacre and lax attention to the threat of terrorism living in their own back yards.

Their tendency to be *"laid back"* is evident with things like Napoleon. He takes them over in the Napoleonic war. In the 1800's at war with England, as the firstborn of Israel's they lose the birthright to Napoleon.

---

[34] *Genesis 49:8-12 Judah, thou art he whom thy brethren shall praise: thy hand shall be in the neck of thine enemies; thy father's children shall bow down before thee. (9) Judah is a lion's whelp: from the prey, my son, thou art gone up: he stooped down, he couched as a lion, and as an old lion; who shall rouse him up? (10) The scepter shall not depart from Judah, nor a lawgiver from between his feet, until Shiloh come; and unto him shall the gathering of the people be. (11) Binding his foal unto the vine, and his ass's colt unto the choice vine; he washed his garments in wine, and his clothes in the blood of grapes: (12) His eyes shall be red with wine, and his teeth white with milk.*

***Deuteronomy 33:1** And this is the blessing, wherewith Moses the man of God blessed the children of Israel before his death.*

Of all the western nations, France has the lowest birthrate, although they outnumber England 6 to 1.

These two are lumped together and are scattered among the other nations of Israel. They are never assigned a portion of land for their inheritance because of their lack of anger management among their brethren.

[35]**SIMEON.** His people are scattered. They are among all the modern nations of Israel without specific identity. In fact, Moses does not even mention them as a tribe! Because God inspires Jacob to pronounce, they are to be scattered among Israel. This happens when Israel splits into two major factions. They are in Palestine south of Judah, but when the split happens, they leave with the other 10 tribes of Israel.

LEVI. This is the priestly tribe and is also scattered throughout Israel. They are never assigned land as an inheritance. The name Levi, Levy, and Levine are found in the tribes of Judah a lot. Also, Cohen and its variations. In **Hebrew Kohan** means priest and is translated 723 times that way. They are scattered among Judah because they lose their priestly functions in Israel totally. Jeroboam causes that when he is king.

***1Kings 12:31** And he made a house of high places, and made priests of the lowest of the people, which were not of the sons of Levi.*

EXPLANATION OF THE TERM JEWS

[36]**JUDAH**. Not to be confused with the term **JEWS**. This is a good place to explain the difference in Judah and Jews. Jews is the name first applied to the people who dwelt in ancient land of Judah! This was when Israel divided into two kingdoms of Israel and Judah. *(This happened after*

---

[35] ***Romans 2:28-29*** *For he is not a Jew, which is one outwardly; neither is that circumcision, which is outward in the flesh:*
(29) ***But he is a Jew, which is one inwardly****; and circumcision is that of the heart,* ***in the spirit****, and not in the letter; whose praise is not of men, but of God.*
[36] ***Genesis 49:13*** *Zebulun shall dwell at the haven of the sea; and he shall be for a haven of ships; and his border shall be unto Zidon.*

the days of King Solomon) It wasn't until after the 70 year of captivity Judah and Benjamin the descendants of Abraham were called "Jews".

The term **Jews is applied in the New Testament for all Israelites opposed to** *the "Gentiles."* It is a religious term not an ethnic identification. [37]Paul refers to the Jews in this manner when speaking of the person who is pleasing God.

In modern times Jews, have become known as those who do not accept Jesus Christ has come as the Messiah. Since the Jewish leadership were hostile toward Jesus' ministry, they are sometimes confused with the ethnic label of the people called Jews who were God's chosen people. In that sense, he was identifying the difference between **Jews and pagans**. All the apostles eventually adopt the term *"Israelites"* to mean followers of Judeo/Christian teachings. In the early days of the church, most congregations were made up of believing Jews mixed with Gentile peoples. Especially in Paul's missionary travels. Some accept Christ others denying the Messiah has come yet.

In these modern times, many see Israel as Jewish. **It is now a religious term for the faith of the people of Israel or anyone choosing this belief.** The people are often referred to as Israelis. In modern times, there are few ethnic people of Judah in Israel. There are some in Denmark and a lot of them migrated to England.

The Hapsburgs and the royal line of Queen Elizabeth are from the lineage of Judah.

[38]**ZEBULUN.** His people settled in **HOLLAND** (Netherlands). They are a colonizing people dwelling at the "shore of the sea."

[39]**ISSACHAR** The people of **FINLAND**. They are a hardworking people. They have paid off a huge debt to Russia over the years. Their wealth comes from fishing and glass making.

---

[37] ***Genesis 49:14-15*** *Issachar is a strong ass couching down between two burdens: (15) And he saw that rest was good, and the land that it was pleasant; and bowed his shoulder to bear and became a servant unto tribute.*

[38] ***Genesis 49:16-18*** *Dan shall judge his people, as one of the tribes of Israel. (17) Dan shall be a serpent, an adder in the path, which bite the horse heels, so that his rider shall fall backward. (18) I have waited for thy salvation, O LORD*

[39] ***Genesis 49:19*** *Gad, a troop shall vercome him: but he shall overcome at the last*

⁴⁰**DAN. DENMARK** and the **DANES**! The ancient tribe of Dan was originally divided into two parts, one about Joppa, a seaport, and the other in the north of Palestine. Dan ruled his own people independent of Israel's kings. Down through history they acquired the lands of Virgin Islands, Greenland, Iceland, and other islands in their "hey day."

⁴¹**GAD.** Modern day **SWITZERLAND.** The only nation where every man is mobilized for defense. They are a nation of troops. It is no accident that the Geneva Conference is there.

⁴²**ASHER.** Modern day **BELGIUM.** ASHER is sometimes confused with ASSUR. The twin brother of ARAXPHAD in history.

From ASHER'S lineage, we have the finest Flemish paintings, the royal tapestries which grace the halls of kings, fine out diamonds, porcelain, and Belgian lace.

Because of oil reserves and huge Uranium deposits, Belgium is wealthy and will continue to prosper and grow as a nation. Could be why so many of the current day ISIS terrorist "cells" hide out there to form operations.

⁴³**NAPHTALI** is modern day **SWEDEN.** From SWEDEN come the Nobel prizes in token of great world accomplishments. She is renowned for sending emissaries to speak words of peace and conciliation.

---

40 ***Genesis 49:20*** *Out of Asher his bread shall be fat, and he shall yield royal dainties.* ***Deuteronomy 33:24-25*** *And of Asher he said, Let Asher be blessed with children; let him be acceptable to his brethren, and <u>let him dip his foot in oil</u>. (25) Thy shoes shall be iron and brass; and as thy days, so shall thy strength be.*
41 G***enesis 49:21*** *Naphtali is a hind let loose: he giveth goodly words.*
42 ***Genesis 49:27*** *Benjamin shall raven as a wolf: in the morning, he shall devour the prey, and at night he shall divide the spoil.*
43 ***Genesis 49:22-26*** *Joseph is a fruitful bough, even a fruitful bough by a well; <u>whose branches run over the wall</u>: (23) The archers have sorely grieved him, and shot at him, and hated him: (24) <u>But his bow abode in strength</u>, and the arms of his hands were made strong by the hands of the mighty God of Jacob; (from thence is the shepherd, the stone of Israel:) (25) Even by the God of thy father, who shall help thee; and by <u>the Almighty, who shall bless thee with blessings of heaven above, blessings of the deep that lies under</u>, blessings of the breasts, and of the womb: (26) The blessings of thy father have prevailed above the blessings of my progenitors unto the utmost bound of the everlasting hills: they shall be on the head of Joseph, and on the crown of the head of him that was separate from his brethren*

⁴⁴**BENJAMIN** is modern day **NORWAY and ICELAND.** The smallest of the tribes and this is still true today. There are fewer Norwegians than any other group today.

JOSEPH's sons; Ephraim and Manasseh

⁴⁵**JOSEPH** is a whole different story when it comes to the tribes of Israel. This is because of how he is separated from his brethren because of the favor of God upon him and the jealousy of his brethren. Joseph is also found in academic history under his Egyptian name, Sophis. He was an Egyptian Pharaoh over the Southern Delta. This gives Joseph pre-eminence above the other Israelites nations even to this day. He represents in modern times both **ENGLAND** and **the UNITED STATES OF AMERICA.** The national blessings are bestowed upon Joseph's two sons.

EPHRIAM AND MANASSEH.

Genesis 48:3-20 And Jacob said unto Joseph, God Almighty appeared unto me at Luz in the land of Canaan, and blessed me, (4) And said unto me, Behold, I will make thee fruitful, and multiply thee, and I will make of thee a multitude of people; and will give this land to thy seed after thee for an everlasting possession. (5) And now thy two sons, **Ephraim, and Manasseh***, which were born unto thee in the land of Egypt before I came unto thee into Egypt, are mine; as Reuben and Simeon, they shall be mine. (6) And thy issue, which thou begot after them, shall be thine, and shall be called after the name of their brethren in their inheritance. (7) And as for me, when I came from Padan, Rachel died by me in the land of Canaan in the way, when yet there was but a little way to come unto Ephrath: and I buried her there in the way of Ephrath; the same is Bethlehem. (8) And Israel beheld Joseph's sons, and said, who are these? (9) And Joseph said unto his father, they are my sons, whom God hath given me in this place. And he said, bring them, I pray thee, unto me, and I will bless them. (10) Now the eyes of Israel were dim for age, so that he could not see. And he brought them near unto him; and he kissed them and embraced them. (11) And Israel said unto Joseph, I had not thought to see thy*

---

⁴⁴   *2Kings 17:6* In the ninth year of Hoshea the **king of Assyria took Samaria**, and **carried Israel away into Assyria**, and placed them in Halah and in Habor by the river of Gozan, and in the cities of the Medes.

⁴⁵   Genesis 15:13 And he said unto Abram, Know of a surety that thy seed shall be a stranger in a land that is not theirs, and shall serve them; and ***they shall afflict them four hundred years;***

face: and, lo, God hath shewed me also thy seed. (12) And Joseph brought them out from between his knees, and he bowed himself with his face to the earth. (13) And Joseph took them both, Ephraim in his right hand toward Israel's left hand, and Manasseh in his left hand toward Israel's right hand and brought them near unto him. (14) And Israel stretched out his right hand, and laid it upon Ephraim's head, who was the younger, and his left hand upon Manasseh's head, guiding his hands wittingly; for Manasseh was the firstborn. (15) And he blessed Joseph, and said, God, before whom my father's Abraham and Isaac did walk, the God which fed me all my life long unto this day, (16) The Angel which redeemed me from all evil, bless the lads; and let my name be named on them, and the name of my father's Abraham and Isaac; and let them grow into a multitude in the midst of the earth. (17) And when Joseph saw that his father laid his right hand upon the head of Ephraim, it displeased him: and he held up his father's hand, to remove it from Ephraim's head unto Manasseh's head. (18) And Joseph said unto his father, not so, my father: for this is the firstborn; put thy right hand upon his head. (19) And his father refused, and said, I know it, my son, I know it: he also shall become a people, and he also shall be great: but truly his younger brother shall be greater than he, and his seed shall become a multitude of nations. (Great Britain before 1960) *(20) And he blessed them that day, saying, in thee shall Israel bless, saying, God make thee as Ephraim and as Manasseh: and he set Ephraim before Manasseh.*

It is significant that the firstborn receives the birthright blessings of the family. But in many cases throughout the bible, we see the birthright transferred for assorted reasons. This is also the case with Ephraim and Manasseh. Also, with Assur and Araxphad.

In the playing out of these blessing to our recent world history, guess who is the Nation on whom the sun never set on their territories and resources? Great Britain! *"His seed shall become a multitude of nations"* Only until shortly after the post-World War Two era the Brits are the largest one nation of nations scattered over the earth. Today this is not true. Sadly, they have fallen into the same apostasy as their forefathers, Israel, often did and lost their favor in the eyes of God. No other country fits this scenario but England, or once known as Great Britain. Therefore, **EPHRAIM** is modern day **ENGLAND** our longest and closest ally.

This leaves the first-born brother **MANASSEH**. This must be **AMERICA**. He is also destined to become a great nation. America sets on the most diverse and bountiful natural resources of any other nation or country in the world! America's rise to power has made us the *"go to nation,"* most *"looked up to for world leadership"* country in the world. We are the most powerful nation in the world, post-World War Two.

Sadly, this is becoming no longer true. We have allowed our founding principles to be compromised and diminished to the point of indebtedness to many other nations.

What God warns ancient Israel would happen if they forsook Him is happening to America. Our money still says, *"In God We Trust"* but our open culture and political correctness speaks louder and louder each day. We tolerate other cultures to the extent that our own identity as Americans is threatened. That is a story for another book.

Many of the ancient nations retain their original names. Nations such as Egypt, Libya, Ethiopia, and Greece just to name a few.

GENTILE NATIONS IDENTIFIED

I will list a few of the other nations that can be identified in modern times by their ancient original names. This is for prophetic understanding of the nations involved in the end-time prophesies. I especially want you to understand the meaningful relationship Germany will have during the Great Tribulation.

Austria = Asshur Germany= Asshur

Note: This is a different **Asshur** from the Israelite Tribe **Asher**. These are the descendants of Asshur who the twin brother of Araxphad Shem's sons is. Asher the Israelite comes through Araxphad's lineage. Assyrians come through Asshur, his twin brother.

Most of these are descendants of Ham and Japheth the other sons of Noah.

Gog and Magog = Russia and China Korea = Gomer, Magog
Edom = Turkey **Japan** = Gomer **Libya** = Miziaram
Italy = Chaldean, Javan **Jordan** = Ammon, Moab
Lebanon = Uz **Colombia** = Tarshish **Hungary** = Keturah
Costa Rica= Tarshish **Iceland** = Benjamin
Crete, Isle = Caphtor **India** = Phut, Cush
Cuba = Tarshish **Indo-China** = Gomer
The Czech Republic = Elam **Indonesia** = Gomer
Iran = Persians Iraq = Ammon, Moab

COMBINING ASSUR AND ARAXPHAD LEGACY

Now let's move up in history to about the same time **Assur's** descendants, the **Assyrians,** were reidentified as **Germans**. This was about **612 B.C.** when the Scythians and other tribes overtook the **Assyrian Empire**. By this time **Araxphad's** descendants, the **Israelites**, were a divided nation. Then 8 years after the Assyrian Empire's destruction, the Jews, (*Judah and Benjamin*) were taken from their land as captives to **Babylon**. [46]A few years before the Jews were exported to Babylon, the other 10 tribes of Israelites were deported beyond the Euphrates River by the **Assyrian king Shalmaneser.**

I believe about this time in history is when God began to allow the descendants of Shem, Ham, and Japheth to connect with each other on a national platform.

This is where prophecy begins to come alive in fulfillment once again since the days of Abraham, Moses, and the Israelites. [47]Remember the

---

[46] Exodus 12:**41 *And it came to pass at the end of the four hundred and thirty years***, even the selfsame day it came to pass, that all ***the hosts of the LORD went out from the land of Egypt.***

[47] Acts 7:2-6 And he said, Men, brethren, and fathers, hearken; The God of glory appeared unto our father Abraham, when he was in Mesopotamia, before he dwelt in Charran,

(3) And said unto him, Get thee out of thy country, and from thy kindred, and come into the land which I shall shew thee.

(4) Then came he out of the land of the Chaldaeans, and dwelt in Charran: and from thence, when his father was dead, he removed him into this land, wherein ye now dwell.

(5) And he gave him none inheritance in it, no, not so much as to set his foot on: yet he promised that he would give it to him for a possession, and to his seed after him, when as yet he had no child.

*(6) And God spoke on this wise, That his seed should sojourn in a strange land; and that **they should bring them into bondage, and entreat them evil four hundred years.***

prophecy of Israel being in bondage for four hundred years? [48]It happened! [49]Remember when God chose Abraham and his descendants, the Israelites the prophecy? These prophesies were fulfilled to the near day.

By the year **604 B.C.** the nation of Babylon conquers the nation of Israel (*specifically Judah*) and relocates its people to Babylon. God uses this event to expose the "*heathenistic*" Babylonians to the ways of the invisible God of Israel.

Ironically, after all these centuries, the descendants of Araxphad end up right back in Babylon!

God's chosen nation Israel fails to govern itself by the moral laws God covenants with them. God allows them to be taken away into 70 years of captivity. [50]This Babylonian captivity is a prophesied event by the prophet Jeremiah! It becomes a reality, demonstrating the power of prophecy by the word of God. The prophet Jeremiah delivers this prophecy one hundred years before it happens!

---

[48] *Jeremiah 25:11 And this whole land shall be a desolation, and an astonishment; and these nations shall <u>serve the king of Babylon seventy years</u>.*
Jeremiah 25:12 And it shall come to pass, when seventy years are accomplished, that I will punish the king of Babylon, and that nation, says the LORD, for their iniquity, and the land of the Chaldeans, and will make it perpetual desolations.
Jeremiah 29:10 For thus says the LORD, that <u>after seventy years be accomplished at Babylon</u> I will visit you, and perform my good word toward you, in causing you to return to this place.

[49] **Genesis 15:13-14**
(13) And he said unto Abram, Know of a surety that thy seed shall be a stranger in a land that is not theirs, and shall serve them; **and they shall afflict them four hundred years;**
(14) And also that nation, whom they shall serve, will I judge: and afterward shall they come out with great substance.

[50] **Colossians 2:16-22** *Let no man therefore judge you in meat, or in drink, or in respect of a holyday, or of the new moon, or of the Sabbath days: (17) Which are a shadow of things to come; but the body is of Christ. (18) Let no man beguile you of your reward in a voluntary humility and worshipping of angels, intruding into those things which he hath not seen, vainly puffed up by his fleshly mind, (19) And not holding the Head, from which all the body by joints and bands having nourishment ministered, and knit together, increases with the increase of God. (20)* **Wherefore if ye be dead with Christ from the rudiments of the world, why, as though living in the world, are ye subject to ordinances,** *(21) (Touch not; taste not; handle not; (22) Which all are to perish with the using;)* **after the commandments and doctrines of men**?

There is no way men orchestrate this event. Communication alone, would take weeks and months to set it up. There are too many *"variables"* involved to deliver this event and duration by the plans of men. The captivity involving thousands of people, during a time when communication between nations takes weeks and months to deliver messages, makes it impossible by the work of men.

In today's world of technology, a *"flash mob"* can be created over the internet. Minutes later, thousands of people suddenly appear in an event. It could not have been planned and initiated to conquer and move a nation of people from their home to Babylon. It was prophesied through the prophet Jeremiah by the invisible God.

Without detail this is where I believe some of the descendants of **Assur** and **Araxphad** meet. This is also where the book of Daniel is a huge light upon the kingdoms of mankind from God's viewpoint.

It should be noted that the years prior to this captivity, Israel was constantly at war with various Assyrian nations. Because of their disobedience to God, He allowed these calamities to happen to them. This is the point in time when the tribes of Israel are scattered all over the known world.

CHAPTER TWO

GOD'S RELIGIOUS SYSTEM AND GOVERNMENT FOR ISRAEL THE FOUNDATIONAL FOOTPRINT OF THE PLAN OF GOD FOR MANKIND

God chose the **12 tribes of Israel** to become a nation that He could use to witness His laws and ways to the other nations of the world. [51]He then delivered them from the bondage of the Egyptians as prophesied to Abraham.

During the days before Israel's deliverance from Egypt, God began to teach the Israelites the plan of redemption for mankind. This was God's form of government before the Jews later corrupted it themselves. These holy days began with a ritual observed as a type of the coming Messiah. It was all a physical ritual depicting the actual coming event. The ritual involved the sacrifice of a perfect lamb. The detail is amazing! The timing

---

[51] *Deuteronomy 7:6-8*
(6) For thou art an holy people unto the LORD thy God: the LORD thy God hath chosen thee to be a special people unto himself, above all people that are upon the face of the earth.
(7) The LORD did not set his love upon you, nor choose you, because ye were more in number than any people; for ye were the fewest of all people:
(8) But because the LORD loved you, and because he would keep the oath which he had sworn unto your fathers, hath the LORD brought you out with a mighty hand, and redeemed you out of the house of bondmen, from the hand of Pharaoh king of Egypt.

prematurely matched the actual event when Christ was fulfilling it over a century and a half later.

The Lamb was to be selected on the 10th day of the first month. A lamb of the first year, without blemish, a male. *(Christ came into Jerusalem on the back of a colt on the 10th of Nisan 30 A.D. being lauded as the emancipator of the Jews.)* It was to be kept until the evening of the 14th and then slain. *(Jesus was crucified on the evening of the 14th as the sun was setting in the west and the 15th was beginning)* Its blood painted over and on the door posts of the residences of the Israelites. Its meat was to be cooked and eaten that night by all the family associated to that specific lamb. There were multiple lambs slain, one for each family. All this ritual was relayed by Moses and Aaron as the events were unfolding regarding the impending arrival of the "death angel" to slay the firstborn of any who were not behind the blood sacrifice painted over and on the door post of the houses where they lived.

The Israelites were to eat all the lamb, fully dressed in clothes that were suitable for travel. They were to be packed and ready to travel on a moment's notice from Moses.

It should be noted that this real time event was to be memorialized from that time, every year the anniversary of the event came around. An ordinance forever. The next year and every year after it were to be remembered and become a 7-day festival of eating unleavened bread to commemorate the freedom of bondage for ancient Israel and their escape from living in the bondage of sin each day. The spiritual significance of the ritual was not understood until Christ came to earth and fulfilled its meaning in 30 A.D. At that time, 24 hours the evening before the ancient ritual was to be performed, Jesus sat down with His disciples and changed the symbolic killing of an unblemished lamb, to wine *(Symbolic of His blood shed)* and un-leavened bread. *(Symbolic of His body broken for our healing)* This is because within 24 hours of their Passover dinner, He would become the actual Lamb of God sacrifice prophesied for hundreds of years.

The annual Festivals and Holy Days are commanded to ancient Israel by God to teach them about the salvation Plan of God for mankind. They are physical rituals for ancient Israel to observe, as shadows of actual events relating to the Plan of God for mankind. Jesus raises these judgments to a spiritual level of understanding when He dies.

I write about these annual Holy Days to show the accuracy of prophecy. These Holy Days have not all been fulfilled at this time. Only the coming of Christ the first time and the sending of the Holy Spirit to mankind after Christ's resurrection have been fulfilled. **This means that the other memorial Holy Days are part of the End-Time Prophetic scenario!**

During the days of the Apostle Paul's work in the 1st century churches of the "*new faith*" in Jesus Christ, suffer persecution from the establishment Jews. They are clinging to the "*Old Covenant*" judgments and ordinances God gave Moses. [52]Paul: (See Footnote)

This will take some time to explain but will give you a "*foundational footprint*" of the plan of God for our choices leading us to one of two destinies. I will reveal the details of the annual festivals and Holy Days by going to the book of Leviticus, specifically the 23rd chapter.

Leviticus 23:4 *These are the feasts of the LORD, even holy convocations, which ye shall proclaim in their seasons.*

These annual festivals are to be an annual reminder of Israel's physical deliverance from the bondage of being slaves to the Egyptians. They are meant to be a physical ritual memorializing the events, past and future for the people of God. This process is judgment from God to physically teach ancient Israel about God's plan for spiritual salvation when the Messiah has come and fulfilled the first part of this plan.

Though the children of Israel do not have spiritual understanding of these rituals; they are under the physical consequences of God's punishment if they simply ignore them. This becomes evident throughout their history as a nation. Ancient Israel suffers captivities and eventual scattering of their peoples into other nations of the world. This process ended in **1948 A. D.** with the establishment of Israel as a nation returning to the specific territory promised to them.

The establishment of the ritual observance of the plan begins on the night before Israel's departure from Egypt. <u>Remember, ancient Israel is all about physical salvation from death.</u> I will try to keep this as brief as possible. You could read the complete story in the book of Exodus chapters 1-14. The first major event in completing Israel's deliverance is important because it foreshadows the prophesied Messiah's sacrifice for deliverance

---

[52] **Psalms 103:12** *As far as the east is from the west, so far hath he removed our transgressions from us.*

from sins of all who accept Him as the Savior and Son of God. What God tells Israel to do, prior to and on the night before they are set free from the bondage of Egypt is a typology of the *"Lamb of God,"* Jesus of Nazareth, who will give His life 1,500 years later.

It is a lengthy read, but it is important in establishing the spiritual foundation for why Christians believe and worship Jesus Christ. It also creates a foundational footprint for the Plan of God. This event in ancient Israel's history is **physical typology** for the **spiritual concept** of redemption that is fulfilled by Christ 1500 years later. You may wonder how this relates to end-time events ahead of us. This is because everything and every prophecy in the Old Testament points to the coming Messiah to provide spiritual salvation for us. Much of what Jesus teaches is the establishment of the Kingdom of God on this earth upon His return the second time at the end of Armageddon! Holy Days are prophetic for the end times also. We are now in church era.

The biblical scenario you are about to read is the very beginning of this process that God has planned for the redemption of mankind. It is first physical ordinances of worship required of the Israelites. [53](God's chosen people) These physical religious rituals portray various stages of God's plan for mankind's salvation. It is based on their physical salvation until Christ comes to fulfill the typology represented by the sacrificial lamb. When Jesus is sacrificed, and the Holy Spirit is sent to those who believe in Jesus, these festivals and Holy days become the prophetic spiritual understanding of events leading up to eternal salvation for mankind. When we accept Jesus, as the guiding force in our daily lives, the Holy Spirit will influence our minds to understand the Plan of God reflected by these physical holy days.

Exodus 12:1-5 *And the LORD spoke unto Moses and Aaron in the land of Egypt, saying, (2) This* ***month shall be unto you the beginning of months:*** *it shall be the first month of the year to you. (3) Speak ye unto all the congregation of Israel, saying, In the* ***tenth day of this month*** *they shall* ***take to them every man a lamb****, according to the house of their fathers,* ***a lamb for a house****: (4) And if the household be too little for the lamb, let him and his neighbor next unto his house take it per the number of the souls; every man according to his eating shall make your count for the lamb. (5) Your*

---

[53] **Leviticus 23:1-44**

*lamb shall be without blemish, a male of the first year: ye shall **take it out from the sheep:***

Exodus 12:6-7** And ye **shall keep it up until the fourteenth day of the same month: and the whole assembly of the congregation of Israel shall kill it in the evening.** (7) And they shall **take of the blood and strike it on the two side posts and on the upper door post of the houses, wherein they shall eat it.

> Several points here:
> - God set up the time of the first month.
> - On the 10th day of the month a lamb was to be selected.
> - It was to be a male.
> - Without blemish or any deficiency.
> - Keep it until the 14th of the same month.
> - Kill it in the evening.
> - Put some of its blood over and upon the doorposts of your house.
> - Eat all of it that night.

***Exodus 12:11-28** And thus shall ye eat it; **with your loins girded,** your **shoes on your feet,** and your **staff in your hand;** and ye shall **eat it in haste: it is the LORD'S Passover.** (12) For I will pass through the land of Egypt this night and will smite all the firstborn in the land of Egypt, both man and beast; and against all the gods of Egypt **I will execute judgment: I am the LORD.** (13) And the blood shall be to you for a token upon the houses where ye are and **when I see the blood, I will <u>pass over you</u>,** (This where the term Passover comes from) and the plague shall not be upon you to destroy you, when I smite the land of Egypt. (14) And **this day shall be unto you for a memorial;** and ye shall keep it a feast to the **LORD throughout your generations;** ye shall **keep it a feast by an ordinance forever.** (15) **Seven days shall ye eat unleavened bread;** even the first day ye shall **put away leaven out of your houses:** for whosoever eats leavened bread from the first day until the seventh day, **that soul shall be cut off from Israel.** (16) And in the **first day there shall be a holy convocation,** and in **the seventh day there shall be a holy convocation to you;** no manner of work* shall be done in them, save that which every man must eat, that only may be done of you. (17) **And ye shall observe the feast of unleavened bread; for in this selfsame day have I brought your armies out of the land of Egypt: therefore, shall ye observe this day in your generations by an ordinance forever**. (18) In the first month, on the fourteenth day of the month at even, ye shall eat unleavened bread, until the one and twentieth day of the month at even. (19) **Seven days shall there be no leaven found in your houses: for whosoever eats that which is leavened, even that soul shall be cut off from the congregation of Israel**, whether he be a stranger, or born in the land. (20) **Ye shall eat nothing leavened**; in all **your habitations, shall ye eat unleavened bread**. (21) Then Moses called for all the elders of Israel, and said unto them, draw out and take you a lamb per your families, and kill the Passover. (22) And ye shall take a bunch of hyssops, and dip it in the blood that is in the basin and strike the lintel and the two side posts with the blood that is in the basin; and none of you shall go out at the door of his house until the morning. (23) For the LORD, will pass through to smite the Egyptians; and when he sees the blood upon the lintel, and on the two side posts, the LORD will pass over the door, and will not suffer the destroyer to come in unto your houses to smite you. (24) And ye shall observe this thing for an ordinance to thee and to thy sons forever. (25) And it shall come to pass, when ye be come to the land which the LORD will give you, according as he hath promised, that ye shall keep this service. (26) And it shall come to pass, when your children shall say unto you, what mean ye by this service? (27) That ye shall say, it is the sacrifice of the LORD'S Passover, who passed over the houses of the children of Israel in Egypt, when he smote the Egyptians, and **delivered our houses**. And the people bowed the head and worshipped. (28) And the children of Israel went away and did as the LORD had commanded Moses and Aaron, so did they.

Several points to remember from this scenario of physical events.

- ➢ The children of Israel are warned that the last plague upon Egypt will be a death angel coming to slay all the firstborn of the Egyptians and of their cattle.
- ➢ The following ritual is established to teach Israel their God will deliver them from physical death if they obey the ordinances set before them by Moses and Aaron.

- ➤ This is the beginning of at least 1500 years of physical rituals God will use to teach His plan of redemption for mankind.
- ➤ This is the _old covenant_ with mankind until the Messiah appears upon the earth to fulfill the ultimate sacrifice for sins of mankind.
- ➤ Jesus Christ replaces these rituals when comes to earth and teaches the gospel.
- ➤ What Jesus does by His teaching and sending the Holy Spirit, establishes a _new covenant_ with mankind.
- ➤ The following scripture is what separates the rituals from the new covenant.

Luke 16:14-16 And the Pharisees also, who were covetous, heard all these things: and they derided Jesus. (15) And Jesus said unto them, Ye are they which justify yourselves before men; but God knows your hearts: for the highly esteemed among men is an abomination in the sight of God. (16) **The law and the prophets were until John: since that time, the kingdom of God is preached, and every man presses into it.**

This is when **Jesus elevates the laws for physical rituals to a spiritual understanding** and **puts them in our hearts to remember.** This is also a prophecy from the Old Testament.

Jeremiah 31:31-34 Behold, the days come, says the LORD, that I will make a **_new covenant_** with the house of Israel, and with the house of Judah: (32) **Not according to the covenant that I made with their fathers in the day that I took them by the hand to bring them out of the land of Egypt;** which my covenant they broke, although I was an husband unto them, says the LORD: (33) But this shall be the covenant that I will make with the house of Israel; After those days, says the LORD, **I will put my law in their inward parts, and write it in their hearts;** and will be their God, and they shall be my people. (34) And they shall teach no more every man his neighbor, and every man his brother, saying, Know the LORD: for they shall all know me, from the least of them unto the greatest of them, says the LORD: [54] **for I will forgive their iniquity**, and **I will remember their sin no more.**

---

[54] **Daniel 2:38 KJV.** .and wheresoever the children of men dwell, the beasts of the field and the fowls of the heaven hath he given into thine hand, and hath made thee ruler over them all. **Thou art this head of gold.**

Here are some high points of what is to happen in the first part of God's plan for mankind. It is a physical act that portrays the coming Messiah who would save mankind with His shed blood for sin.

- A lamb of one year old, without blemish is to be selected on the 10th day of the 1st month.
- The lamb is to be kept up until the 14th day of the same month and slain in the evening (evening meant the hours between 3 and 6 P. M.) and the whole congregation shall witness the slaying; the lambs are slain by the elders or head of each home; one for each household.
- They are to stay in their homes, roast and eat the lamb with unleavened bread.
- They are to eat unleavened bread for the following 7 days; the first day is to be a Holy Day and the last day is to be a Holy Day.
- They are to strike the doorposts and lentil of their homes with the blood from the slain lamb.
- This will be a sign to the death angel to Passover their home and not kill them.
- All the firstborn of Egyptians was slain that night, Deaths included **Merenre I** the firstborn of **Neferkare**. It is the last plague God put upon the Egyptians before their freedom is granted by Pharaoh **Merenre-Antyemzaef**, 1488-1487 B. C. His reign is short because he ends up being drown in the Red Sea while chasing the Israelites!

Exodus 14:27-30 *And Moses stretched forth his hand over the sea, and the sea returned to his strength when the morning appeared; and the Egyptians fled against it; and the LORD overthrew the Egyptians in the middle of the sea. (28) And the waters returned, and covered the chariots, and the horsemen, and all the host of Pharaoh that came into the sea after them; there remained not so much as one of them. (29) But the children of Israel walked upon dry land in the middle of the sea; and the waters were a wall unto them on their right hand, and on their left. (30) Thus, the LORD saved Israel that day out of the hand of the Egyptians; and Israel saw the Egyptians dead upon the seashore.*

THE EXODUS

Most everyone is familiar with the story of the Israelites, (Abraham's seed) and how they were delivered from slavery of the Egyptians. The epic film, The Ten Commandments, is an effort to present the story of this event. Now notice the next scriptures.

Exodus 12:40-41 *Now the sojourning of the children of Israel, who dwelt in Egypt, was four hundred and thirty years. (41) And it came to pass at the end of the four hundred and thirty years, even the selfsame day it came to pass, that all the hosts of the LORD went out from the land of Egypt.*

The events leading up to this <u>freedom and departure from Egypt is the significant beginning of the *physical portrayal*</u> of the redemption plan of God for all of mankind! The Israelites were lead from slavery to freedom as a type of redemption from sin to righteousness.

God memorializes the details of the physical process for the next 1500 years in His instructions to the Israelites at Mount Sinai as He covenants with the Israelites. God will bless them for obedience and curse them for disobedience. The next part of this story is especially important for today's Christian to understand. I will be as brief as possible, but please spend some time with the books of Exodus, Leviticus, Numbers, and Deuteronomy as a personal bible study. It did help me see the reason Christ came to us and made a <u>*better covenant*</u> with mankind by raising all this physical typology to a spiritual understanding in worship.

I will cover just the basic commandments and judgements that portray the plan of God for mankind from these physical festivals and Holy Days. The story begins in Exodus Chapter Nineteen.

Exodus 19:1-6 *In the third month, when the children of Israel were gone forth out of the land of Egypt, the same day came they into the wilderness of Sinai. (2) For they were departed from Rephidim, and were come to the desert of Sinai, and had pitched in the wilderness; and there Israel camped before the mount. (3) And Moses went up unto God, and the LORD called unto him out of the mountain, saying, thus shalt thou say to the house of Jacob, and tell the children of Israel; (4) Ye have seen what I did unto the Egyptians, and how I bare you on eagles' wings, and brought you unto Myself. (5) Now therefore, if ye will obey My voice indeed, and keep My covenant, then <u>ye shall be a peculiar</u>*

treasure unto Me above all people: for all the earth is Mine: (6) And ye shall be unto Me a kingdom of priests, and a holy nation. These are the words which thou shalt speak unto the children of Israel.

So, Moses prepares the children of Israel to meet God at the base of Mount Sinai. God thunders out the Ten Commandments. The people are scared and afraid.

Exodus 20:18-21 *And all the people saw the thundering, and the lightnings, and the noise of the trumpet, and the mountain smoking: and when the people saw it, they removed, and stood afar off. (19) And they said unto Moses, speak thou with us, and we will hear but let not God speak with us, lest we die. (20) And Moses said unto the people, Fear not: for God is come to prove you, and that his fear may be before your faces, that ye sin not. (21) And the people stood afar off, and Moses drew near unto the thick darkness where God was.*

Then Moses goes before the Lord and is given *Judgments* for a process of physical worship portraying the plan of God. These are found in the next three chapters, 21, 22, and 23. I will skip to the things pertaining to the prophesies of the plan of God to keep from getting bogged down in the other details of the Judgments of God.

Exodus 23:14-17 *Three times thou shalt keep a feast unto me in the year. (15) Thou shalt keep the feast of unleavened bread: (thou shalt eat unleavened bread seven days, as I commanded thee, in the time appointed of the month Abib; for in it thou came out from Egypt: and none shall appear before me empty:) (16) And the feast of harvest, the first fruits of thy labors, which thou hast sown in the field: and the feast of ingathering, which is in the end of the year, when thou hast gathered in thy labors out of the field. (17) Three times in the year all thy males shall appear before the Lord GOD.*

We are looking at *three seasonal festivals* with *a total of seven special holy days*. These holy days are treated with the same respect as the weekly sabbaths. Now these are just the high points of the three main feasts they are to keep before God.

We will see the details of each of the three a little later. These are "seasonal," one in Spring, Summer, and Fall. I want to now list the three seasonal festivals and the specific Holy Days associated with them for reference.

1. Feast of Unleavened Bread:

I should mention that the Passover observance becomes an annual memorial service celebrated each year before the days of unleavened bread to remember Israel's deliverance from Egypt. The Jews were doing this in the time of Jesus among them. Egypt is biblically a metaphor associated with sin and sinful behavior. The sacrificial lamb is a type of the coming Christ who eventually is born and changes the *old covenant* made with ancient Israel and raising all the laws of God to a spiritual level of understanding. The indwelling of the Holy Spirit of Jesus and the Father God support this. Jesus becomes our high priest; (*Hebrews 7:12 For the priesthood being changed, there is made of necessity a change also of the law.*)

John 14:19-23 *Yet a little while, and the world see me no more; but ye see me: because I live, ye shall live also. (20) At that day ye shall know that I am in my Father, and ye in me,* <u>*and I in you*</u>*. (21) He that hath my commandments, and keeps them, he it is that loves me: and he that loves me shall be loved of my Father, and I will love him, and will manifest myself to him. (22) Judas says unto him, not Iscariot, Lord, how is it that thou wilt manifest thyself unto us, and not unto the world? (23) Jesus answered and said unto him, if a man loves me, he will keep my words: and my Father will love him, and* <u>*we will come unto him, and make our abode with him*</u>*.*

This is accomplished by the indwelling of their Holy Spirit influence upon our mind and will accepting Jesus as our Lord and Master.

On the 15th Day of the 1st month is to be a *Holy Day* observed like the weekly 7th day Sabbath (No servile work and is a day of physical rest from normal activities) in the 10 Commandments. Beginning on that 1st Holy day the Israelites were to eat only unleavened bread. They are to do this for the 5 consecutive days following and through the 7th day of that series is to be a *Holy Day*. This is a total of 7 days of eating unleavened bread. There are other rituals associated which I will explain later. The unleavened bread is a physical symbol of humility; the opposite of being puffed up with leaven or living a sinful life. *Paul gives the spiritual application for this; (1Corinthians 5:8 Therefore let us keep the feast, not with old leaven, neither with the leaven of malice and wickedness; but with the unleavened bread of sincerity and truth.)*

2. Feast of First Fruits:

This is a one-day event to be observed as a Holy Day exactly 50 days counting from the weekly 7th day Sabbath which falls within the physical week of the Feast of Unleavened Bread cycle of days. Again, treated like the weekly 7th day Sabbath with rituals I will explain later.

3. Feast of Ingathering or Tabernacles:

On the 1st day of the 7th month is a *Holy Day*. On the 10th day of the 7th month is a *Holy Day*. On the 15th day of the 7th month is a *Holy Day* followed by 6 days of celebration. On the 22nd day of the 7th month is a *Holy Day*. These days have physical rituals which I will explain later.

We are looking at 3 seasonal festivals with a total of 7 Holy Days to be observed. Now, before I explain the significance of these; let's look at what else God tells Moses to tell the people.

Exodus 23:19-22 *The first of the first fruits of thy land thou shalt bring into the house of the LORD thy God. Thou shalt not seethe a kid in his mother's milk. (20) Behold, I send an Angel before thee, to keep thee in the way, and to bring thee into the place which I have prepared. (21) Beware of him, and obey his voice, provoke him not; for he will not pardon your transgressions: for my name is in him. (22) But if thou shalt indeed obey his voice and do all that I speak; then I will be an enemy unto thine enemies, and an adversary unto thine adversaries.*

> This is part of the national blessings and cursing God promised Israel as they are to inherit the lands, He is giving them as promised to Abraham over 500 years before. God selects the tribe of Levi to be the Priesthood of rulers to oversee the moral education and worship of the other tribes. Through the next 10 chapters of the book of Exodus you can read about how God instructs and sets up this system of physical worship. This is a theocratic government not unlike what the Catholic Church has copied and tried down through the history of Roman Empires.

There is one thing God commanded that is to be a perpetual sign between God and Israel forever. It is an expanded explanation of **the 4th commandment, the 7th day Sabbath of rest.**

Exodus 31:12-18 And the LORD spoke unto Moses, saying, (13) Speak thou also unto the children of Israel, saying, verily my Sabbaths ye shall keep: for it is a sign between me and you throughout your generations; that ye may know that I am the LORD that doth sanctify you. (14) Ye shall keep the Sabbath; therefore, for it is holy unto you: every one that defiles it shall surely be put to death: for whosoever doeth any work therein, that soul shall be cut off from among his people (15) Six days may work be done; but in the seventh is the Sabbath of rest, holy to the LORD: whosoever doeth any work in the Sabbath day, he shall surely be put to death. (16) Wherefore the children of Israel shall keep the Sabbath, to observe the Sabbath throughout their generations, for a perpetual covenant (17<u>*) It is a sign between me and the children of Israel for ever:*</u> *for in six days the LORD made heaven and earth, and on the seventh day he rested, and was refreshed.* (A memorial to creation week) *(18) And he gave unto Moses, when he had made an end of communing with him upon mount Sinai, two tables of testimony, tables of stone, written with the finger of God.*

Therefore, the nation of Israel to this day observes the seventh day of the week as a Holy Day to God. This is the perpetual, that is, uninterrupted in time forever or indefinitely. It is the fourth of the Ten Commandments. The term *"work"* is challenged by the Pharisees during Jesus's time when He picks some corn to eat and even heals someone on the Sabbath Day. Again, history of the Jews tells us they add carnal overzealous ritual to God's Sabbath observance. It is not originally God's intent for such additional commands. Jesus teaches that we should break away from our daily servile work activities and take physical rest with spiritual reflections. Jesus does not restrict practicing charitable deeds and other activities on the sabbath.

These festivals and holy days for ancient Israel are a type of *symbolic memorials* to the plan of God for mankind. They depict some main events that will be markers down through time as the plan develops. Following is a comparison of the ancient festivals and literal plan.

1. Passover Lamb slain = Christ to be the ultimate sacrifice for the sins of mankind. Seven days of eating unleavened bread representing

a life of humility living in the grace of what Christ will do for all of mankind. Seven days of eating unleavened bread as a sign of taking Christ into our conscience and living a Godly life.

2. *1Corinthians 5:6-8 Your glorying is not good. Know ye not that a little leaven leavens the whole lump? (7) Purge out therefore the old leaven, that ye may be a new lump, as ye are unleavened. For even Christ our Passover is sacrificed for us: (8) Therefore let us keep the feast, not with old leaven, neither with the leaven of malice and wickedness; but with the unleavened bread of sincerity and truth.*

3. Feast of First fruits = The people who choose to be first responders to the Holy Spirit of God as it is given to mankind on what is now called the Day of Pentecost. The first time the Holy Spirit is available upon request is in 30 A.D. in the upper room in Jerusalem 50 days after Christ is risen from the dead and seated at the right hand of His Father in heaven. This also is the marker for the beginning of what is commonly called the Church Age. (*Acts 2:1-4 And when the day of Pentecost was fully come, they were all with one accord in one place. (2) And suddenly there came a sound from heaven as of a rushing mighty wind, and it filled all the house where they were sitting. (3) And there appeared unto them cloven tongues like as of fire, and it sat upon each of them. (4) And they were all filled with the Holy Spirit....*)

4. The Feast of Trumpets = **The church age from Christ until He returns**. Trumpets being the main communication for the masses of people in ancient times as a call to listen to what God must say. The <u>preaching of the gospel today</u> is done through mass media instead of trumpet alarms and signals. It is the commission of the church Jesus starts to preach and teach the Gospel of Jesus Christ to all the world. (*Matthew 28:18-20 And Jesus came and spoke unto them, saying, all power is given unto me in heaven and in earth. (19) Go ye therefore, and teach all nations, baptizing them in the name of the Father, and of the Son, and of the Holy Spirit: (20) Teaching them to observe all things whatsoever I have commanded you: and, lo, I am with you always, even unto the end of the world.*)

5. The Day of Atonement = **The binding of Satan for a thousand years when the kingdom of God is established**. In ancient times,

the sins of the people were placed on a goat, metaphorically, and the goat was led into the wilderness and left to wonder. This is depicting blame upon Satan who is constantly trying to undermine the people of God to their destruction. *Revelation 20:1-3 And I saw an angel come down from heaven, having the key to the bottomless pit and a great chain in his hand. (2) And he laid hold on the dragon, that old serpent, which is the Devil, and Satan, and bound him a thousand years, (3) And cast him into the bottomless pit, and shut him up, and set a seal upon him, that he should deceive the nations no more, till the thousand years should be fulfilled: and after that he must be loosed a little season.*

6. Feast of Tabernacles = Known as the feast of ingathering in ancient times. The first day of seven days of observance by living in temporary dwellings. The first day is a holy day representing the 1,000 years of Christ on earth. *Revelation 20:4-5 And I saw thrones, and they sat upon them, and judgment was given unto them: and I saw the souls of them that were beheaded for the witness of Jesus, and for the word of God, and which had not worshipped the beast, neither his image, neither had received his mark upon their foreheads, or in their hands; and they lived and reigned with Christ a thousand years.*

7. The remaining six days represent 1,000 years of generations for each day, from Adam over the next 6,000 years of mankind's dwelling on the earth. People resurrected back to physical life to accept or reject Jesus Christ as their savior. *Revelation 20:5 But the rest of the dead lived not again until the thousand years were finished. This is the first resurrection.*

8. The Last Great Day = The Great White Throne Judgment mentioned in the book of Revelation when God will pass His final judgment upon humanity. *Revelation 20:11-15 And I saw a great white throne, and him that sat on it, from whose face the earth and the heaven fled away; and there was found no place for them. (12) And I saw the dead, small and great, stand before God; and* **the books were opened***: and another book was opened, which is the* **book of life***: and the dead were judged out of those things which were* **written in the books***, according to their works. (13) And the sea gave up the dead which were in it; and death and hell delivered up the*

dead which were in them: and they were judged every man according to their works. (14) And death and hell were cast into the lake of fire. This is the second death. (15) And whosoever was not found written in **the book of life** *was cast into the lake of fire.*

This chapter has outlined the things God uses to teach His people Israel morality and government. The United States adopted most of the judgements you find in the bible as some of the founding fathers searched for laws to govern the new nation. Today there is a likeness of Moses in the legislative chambers that overlooks our government in action. Yet, we suffer from the breaking of many of these laws by our very own elected officials.

During the time of King David and Solomon ruling in Israel, this theocratic type of government worked, and Israel became a great nation. Then a few bad kings came to power and down goes the morality and integrity of good government. Eventually Israel splits into two nations: the Ten Tribes and Judah. The Ten Tribes are taken into captivity and scattered all over the world by their enemies. Judah is eventually taken captive by the Babylonians and moved to Babylon. God used this opportunity to spread His teachings to the Gentile nations and others who did not know the one true God. The book of Daniel is a remarkable story of how the king of Babylon, Nebuchadnezzar learned about the one true God.

The next chapter will outline what the **Gentile nations of men** have developed for their own way of worship and government.

CHAPTER THREE

THE ANCIENT KINGDOMS OF MANKIND

One of many foundational principles to understanding prophecy is knowing that the bible is about the governments of mankind. The bible reveals quite a significant story about the governments of men. The kingdoms of mankind as a worldwide power begins in early **600 B.C.** This **world ruling kingdom** begins with **Nebuchadnezzar of Babylon.** It is revealed to Nebuchadnezzar by a prophetic dream. Since that time, history reveals centuries of kingdoms or nations, one after another, dominating the world until the fall of **Napoleon in 1804 A.D**. Most of history of mankind's government is religious or political war one after another to the present day. This manmade government and lifestyle will be coming to an end when Jesus returns.

The book of Daniel provides foundational information as a timeline of the governments of men. The book of Daniel is a story about God's overall plan to allow mankind to govern itself. It includes many prophesies and the predicted second coming of Jesus Christ! God reveals to Daniel events that will lead to the near destruction of mankind! God uses the prophet Daniel to reveal world ruling influences of governments and empires of men. Daniel's writings are a collection of visionary dreams and angelic appearances. Daniel writes as God reveals events that will create and destroy the empires and governments of men for thousands of years until Christ returns!

During the life of Daniel, we get one of the clearest pictures of **Babylonian** history and events that change King Nebuchadnezzar's life.

His belief in many false gods becomes belief in the One True God. Daniel's position is unique as God uses him and the captivity of his people (*the Jews*) to educate the Gentile nations (*many of the descendants of Assur*) about the intended destiny for mankind.

God chose the nation of Israel, soon after their exodus from Egypt. God establishes a *"moral code"* for Israel as a discipline to govern themselves as a nation. (The Ten Commandments)

The education begins with a set of seasonal rituals becoming the *"footprint"* of God's overall plan that will eventually provide an opportunity for *"Spiritual Salvation."* God gives Israel a set of annual Holy Days to repeat throughout their generations for their "Physical Salvation."

[55]These rituals are *"shadows"* of events to be fulfilled in the "Plan of God" for mankind's salvation as time progresses.

God uses Daniel as a personal witness to the first world ruling king of four other major world kingdoms to come. The fourth kingdom is **Rome.** It has been resurrected several times throughout history and its influence will be a major *"player"* in the end-time new world order before Armageddon. (*Remember that the Romans were the first to call Assyrians Germans.*)

These succeeding Empires are revealed in dream of the king of Babylon, and it is revealed to Daniel by God. This event gives Daniel a prominent position in the Babylonian Empire.

[56]Nebuchadnezzar is the head of Gold representing the World Ruling Kingdom of Babylon. The king is not aware of the worldwide status his power and position in the world has become until Daniel interprets the

---

55 **Daniel 7:1-3** In the first year of Belshazzar king of Babylon Daniel had a dream and visions of his head upon his bed: then he wrote the dream, and told the sum of the matters. (2) Daniel spoke and said, I saw in my vision by night, and, behold, the four winds of the heaven strove upon the great sea. (3) And four great beasts came up from the sea, diverse one from another.

56 **Dan 7:7-8** After this I saw in the night visions, and **behold a <u>fourth beast, dreadful and terrible, and strong exceedingly</u>**; and it had great iron teeth: it devoured and brake in pieces, and stamped the residue with the feet of it: and it was diverse from all the beasts that were before it; and it had ten horns. (8) I considered the horns, and, behold, there came up among them **<u>another little horn</u>**, before whom there were three of the first horns plucked up by the roots: and, behold, in **<u>this horn were eyes like the eyes of man, and a mouth speaking great things</u>**.

dream for him. God uses Daniel to teach the Babylonians His way of life and morality. Much like the story of Joseph and the Pharaoh of Egypt.

THE GREAT IMAGE

As I wrote in my first book, **Why You Were Born**, Daniel was taken captive as a teenager in 604 B.C. along with three of his friends. God brought about circumstances for Daniel to become second in command of the first World Ruling Empire. God used this 70 year of captivity to educate the Gentile nations about the one true God. Also, it was an opportunity for the Jews to have their information put in another language and exposed to the other nations. It was a combining of education opportunities for both the pagans and the Jews.

Let us see what is revealed about the future world ruling kingdoms depicted in this dream of Nebuchadnezzar about the image. This is a *"snapshot"* of the overall scenario of coming world kingdoms after the time of Babylon.

Daniel 2:31-35
(31) Thou, O king, saw, and behold a great image. This great image, whose brightness was excellent, stood before thee; and the form thereof was terrible.
*(32) This image's head was of **fine gold**, his breast and his arms of **silver**, his belly and his thighs of **brass**,*
*(33) His legs of **iron**, his feet part of **iron and part of clay**.*
*(34) Thou saw till **that a stone was cut out without hands**, which **smote the image upon his feet that were of iron and clay**, and brake them to pieces.*
*(35) Then was the iron, the clay, the brass, the silver, and the gold, broken to pieces together, and **became like the chaff of the summer threshing floors; and the wind carried them away, that no place was found for them: and the stone that smote the image became a great mountain, and filled the whole earth.***

The description of the parts of this image and what they are made of covers thousands of years of *history past* and a few short years of *events in our future!*

The **Gold**, **Silver**, **Brass**, **Iron**, and **Iron** mixed with **Clay** represent manmade kingdoms that follow in a progression of time as they are conquered by other kingdoms. You may wonder, how can I say this? Let the bible and academic history tell us. Some of this is history and some of it is prophecy. At the time Daniel penned it most of it was prophecy! Time has since revealed who some of these elements represent as kingdoms.

Below is a representation of these basic kingdoms.

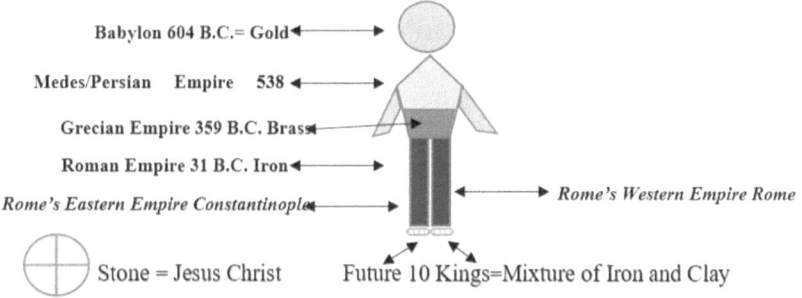

Stone = Jesus Christ Future 10 Kings=Mixture of Iron and Clay
*(34) Thou saw till **that a stone was cut out without hands**, which **smote the image upon his feet that were of iron and clay**, and brake them to pieces.*
*(35) Then was the iron, the clay, the brass, the silver, and the gold, broken to pieces together, and **became like the chaff of the summer threshing floors; and the wind carried them away, that no place was found for them:** and **the stone that smote the image became a great mountain, and filled the whole earth.***

This is an overview of World Kingdoms from 604 B.C. up until the fall of Rome in 476 A.D.

The feet and the stone are predictions for the future ahead of our time. The visionary dream of Nebuchadnezzar revealed by God to Daniel was a "*snapshot*" of World Ruling kingdoms down thru time and into the future ahead of us.

The bible tells us that the **Stone is Jesus**. It is all throughout the bible that **Rock, Stone, Corner Stone, Rock of Ages**, etc., is Metaphor for Jesus. This is metaphoric language predicting the Second Coming of Jesus

Christ to the earth to establish the kingdom of God. These ten toes are a representation of ten ruling kings or leaders that will be influential in the coming New World Order as it develops economically and militarily. They will be subject to the beast power or leader and for a time the "false prophet." This could be the United States of Europe or Common Market Nations with 10 leaders or kings over them. This beast is the "Eighth and of the Seventh" Revelation 17:11

THE FOURTH KINGDOM, ROMAN EMPIRE

For this book, I am going to now concentrate on the Fourth Kingdom of Nebuchadnezzar's dream, The Roman Empire. According to the book of Daniel it is the most terrible and dreaded Empire to ever rise to power.

[57]In the first year of Belshazzar (*Nebuchadnezzar's son*) Daniel gets a vision from God about the kingdoms represented by the Great Image of Nebuchadnezzar's dream. The vision depicted four "beasts" coming up out of the sea. **Sea** is a prophetic metaphor for peoples and nations of the earth.

[58]The fourth beast is the beast that will influence the world for centuries to come. It is the **Roman Empire**. Identified in history by the many resurrections of its powerful leaders for 1260 years after the initial demise of the original Roman Empire. 31 B.C. – 476 A.D. It was during the time of this phase of the Roman Empire that Christ was born and witnessed to the world.

---

[57] **Daniel 7:7-8** After this I saw in the night visions, ***and behold a fourth beast, dreadful and terrible***, and strong exceedingly; and ***it had great iron teeth: it devoured and brake in pieces***, and stamped the residue with the feet of it: and ***it was diverse from all the beasts that were before it; and it had ten horns.*** (8) I considered the horns, and, behold, ***there came up among them another little horn***, before whom there were three of the first horns plucked up by the roots: and***, behold, in this horn were eyes like the eyes of man, and a mouth speaking great things.***

[58] **Daniel 7:24-25** And the ten horns out of this kingdom are ten kings that shall arise: and another shall rise after them; and he shall be diverse from the first, ***and he shall subdue three kings.*** (25) And he shall speak great words against the most High, ***and shall wear out the saints of the most High, and think to change times and laws: and they shall be given into his hand until a time and times and the dividing of time.***

This is where the story gets interesting as we follow the progressions of prophesies connected to this fourth beast. It is the beast power that comes and goes many times down through history and will eventually become the **ten toes** of the Great Image in Daniel chapter two! *(More about that later)*

To follow this Fourth Beast down through history, we must go to several different scriptures and some academic history to identify this beast power.

I will forego the footnotes for a bit, and have you read the scriptures related to this beast.

Daniel 7:23-25 *Thus he said, The* ***fourth beast shall be the fourth kingdom upon earth****, which shall be diverse from all kingdoms, and shall devour the whole earth, and shall tread it down, and break it in pieces.*

The Fourth Kingdom is different from its predecessors.

(24) And the ten horns out of this kingdom are ten kings that shall arise: ***and another shall rise after them; and he shall be diverse from the first, and he shall subdue three kings****.*

There is a time in academic history that matches this scenario. It involves the slow death of the original Roman Empire. This empire came to an end in 476 A.D.

(25) And he shall speak great words against the most High, and shall wear out the saints of the most High, and think to change times and laws: and they shall be given into his hand until a time and times and the dividing of time.

This must be a reference to the Papacy of the Catholic church who influences the beast power down through history.

From the time of the first Popes the Beast power or Fourth Beast has had many faces and tried many times to rule the world.

IDENTIFYING THE ORIGINAL BEAST

Though all these kingdoms were powerful influences upon the earth. [59]The bible tells us that the Fourth Kingdom is the most dreadful and terrible. There are many Old Testament prophesies that bring the book of **Revelation** into focus and understanding. We must be willing to research the Old Testament scriptures and academic history for the answers to the metaphoric language in Revelation. This is an Old Testament writing we must consider as we develop an understanding of the overall prophesies revealing the plans of God for mankind.

Daniel's visionary dream is **about the Fourth Kingdom, Rome. It will have worldwide influence upon the people of the earth for centuries to come and on past our time today.**

[60]Think about how powerful Roman influence has been. The **months, days of the week**, and how days are started and ended have **the Romans changed all.**

In biblical prophetic writings, scholars agree that the word "*horn*" represents a king or powerful leadership. Without boring you with the metaphors of the preceding three world kingdoms I will move to the

---

[59] ***Pope Gregory XIII** (Latin: Gregorius XIII; 7 January 1502 – 10 April 1585), born **Ugo Boncompagni**, was Pope of the Catholic Church from 13 May 1572 to his death in 1585. He is best known for commissioning and being the namesake for the Gregorian calendar, which remains the internationally accepted civil calendar to this day.*

[60] *Daniel 7:19-23)* Then I would know **the truth of the fourth beast**, which was diverse from all the others, exceeding dreadful, whose teeth were of iron, and his nails of brass; which devoured, brake in pieces, and stamped the residue with his feet; (20) And of the ten horns that were in his head, and of **the other which came up, and before whom three fell**; even of **that horn that had eyes, and a mouth that spoke very great things, whose look was more stout than his fellows**. (21) I beheld, and **the same horn made war with the saints, and prevailed against them**; (22) Until the ***Ancient of days came, and judgment was given to the saints of the most High;*** and **the time came that the saints possessed the kingdom**. (23) Thus he said, The fourth beast shall be **the fourth kingdom upon earth, which shall be diverse from all kingdoms**, and shall devour the whole earth, and shall tread it down, and break it in pieces.

Fourth. In Daniel 7:25 is a two-fold prophecy that has been fulfilled once.[61] Pope Gregory changed the calendar.

THE FOURTH KINDOM, THE BEAST WITH SEVEN HEADS & 10 HORNS THE ROMAN EMPIRE

The Roman Empire is described by Daniel's vision from God a diverse from the other kingdoms before it. It is a beastly world power represented by 10 "horns" or rulers. It says that among the first 3 horns were destroyed by a horn that came up among the others. However, this horn is described as having eyes of a man and a mouth that speaks remarkable things. Who could this little horn be?

This is when academic history must come into the foundational information for understanding these visionary prophesies given to Daniel and 500 years later to the Apostle John, the book of Revelation. [62]The largest clue to this beast is that it has worldwide influence that carries from generation to generation.

Without boring you with historical details, I will, *"cut to the chase"* so to speak.

---

[61] *Revelation 13:11-18* And I beheld another beast coming up out of the earth; and he had two horns like a lamb, and **he spoke as a dragon**. (12) And **he exercised all the power of the first beast before him**, and causes the earth and them which dwell therein to worship the first beast, whose deadly wound was healed. (13) And he doeth great wonders, so that he makes fire come down from heaven on the earth in the sight of men, (14) And **deceives them that dwell on the earth by the means of those miracles which he had power to do in the sight of the beast**; saying to them that dwell on the earth, that they should make an image to the beast, which had the wound by a sword, and did live. 15) And he had power to give life unto the image of the beast, that the image of the beast should both speak, and cause that as many as would not worship the image of the beast should be killed. (16) And he causes all, both small and great, rich and poor, free and bond, to receive a mark in their right hand, or in their foreheads: (17) And that no man might buy or sell, save he that had the mark, or the name of the beast, or the number of his name. (18) Here is wisdom. Let him that hath understanding count the number of the beast: for it is the number of a man; and his number is Six hundred threescore and six.

[62] **Acts 2:1** And when the day of Pentecost was fully come, they were all with one accord in one place.

When the official Roman Empire fell in 476 A.D., it was a slow death that took a few hundred years to play out. Eventually the 3 horns that fell brought Rome to its knees only to be out done by the *"little horn"* rising to power. The 3 that fell are:

- The Herili
- The Visigoths
- The Vandals

Guess what? These were all Germanic tribes who turned against Roman government. They were *"rooted out"* and **Justinian** joined forces with the Pope of the Roman Catholic Church! The history of the Popes and the Roman Catholic church has its roots in the later years of the Roman Empire from about 200-300 A.D. this is during the rise of Constantine the so-called *"father of Christianity."* In verse 21 of the footnote, is referring to the time of persecution of the Apostles and Christian believers in Jesus Christ up until the middle age's history.

I don't want to get bogged down with details of history so I will try to be brief.

The KEY INFORMATION for this change in Rome's power is found in the book of Revelation. It involves what theologians call the *"deadly wound."* There are differences of opinion between scholars as to what this was. I will present my understanding in this book.

The similarity of the Revelation 13 beast and Daniel 7 Beast is the 10 horns. Another clue is found in Revelation 13:1. The Beast has Seven Heads. This means nothing until you compare the *"deadly wound"* with other clues. This can get confusing quickly. I will do my best to make sense of it.

Look at the representation below for an overview of the two Roman Empires described in Revelation 13:11.

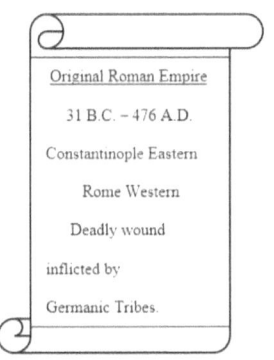 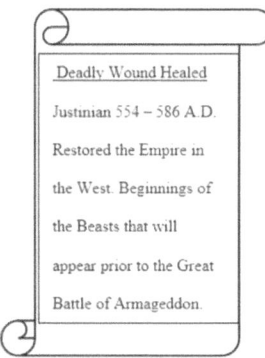

This is confirmation of the "deadly wound healed." The First Horn of this "lamb" is the original Roman Empire before its demise in 476 A.D.

The Second Horn is the Resurrection of the Holy Roman Empire down through history.

[63]These are the TWO horns of the Lamb in Revelation 13:11. The former Roman Empire and its many transitions down through history until the time of Armageddon. I am getting a little ahead of the story, but this is an important revelation about the Fourth Kingdom and its many faces down through history. There will be more information later in chapters.

A SIDEBAR TO THE FOURTH KINGDOM, ROME

After Jesus was crucified, the Apostles were all murdered, and the Church [64]Jesus started with the Apostles on Pentecost was persecuted beyond belief for the next few hundred years. The belief in Jesus was impossible to stop as believers were willing to suffer all sorts of torture even death.

It was Constantine who tied the Catholic Church to the "Beast" and brought the persecution against Christians to a stop in 311A.D. Constantine

---

[63] **Revelation 17:10** And there are seven kings: **five are fallen**, and **one is**, and **the other is not yet come**; and when he cometh, he must continue a short space.

[64] **Daniel 12:4** But thou, O Daniel, shut up the words, and seal the book, **even to the time of the end: many shall run to and fro, and knowledge shall be increased.**

combined the Pagan Mystery Religion of Rome to the Christian efforts established by Jesus and the Apostles. The result is a perverse version of "Christianity."

Constantine's epiphany was not a conversion to Christ, it was a necessity to merge paganism and politics, to Christianity for more power and control of people. **Christianity was tied into government for more control of situations that plagued the Empire.**

Constantine selected Constantinople (modern Istanbul) as his capital in 324 A.D. It was Constantine who made major changes to what Jesus taught and God commanded. Just 46 years later the Germanic tribes crossed the Danube into the Empire, led by the **Visigoths**. One hundred years later, Odovacar, the **Herulian**, deposed Romulus Augustus, ending the Original Roman Empire of five hundred years in power.

This religious power of the church of Rome is untouched and continues right up to the time of Armageddon. Though it seems to disappear at times, it is still on the scene. It is interesting to note that the very people who brought the Roman military power over the world to an end, suddenly become close friends with the Roman Catholics and the Pope. This is a duet that shows up all down through Five of the Seven heads of the Beast.

It is important to keep in mind that the Fourth Beast is a world military power that is overshadowed by the Holy Catholic Church. The Catholic Church is the *"influence that rides the beast and makes it do terrible things."* For example: The Inquisitions against Christians.

[65]There is an interesting passage of scripture in Revelation about these *"heads."*

---

[65]   *Revelation 17:16 And the **ten horns** which thou saw upon the beast, **these shall hate the whore, and shall make her desolate and naked, and shall eat her flesh, and burn her with fire.***

[66]The prophecy is for us in the "latter days" and so the language is not particularly tied to the time of John's writing. A mistake often made by commentaries when interpreting prophecy.

Who are these "***heads***" that come with the healing of the "***deadly wound?***" Who are the "*five who have fallen?*" Who are the "*heads*" that are "*one is.*" Who is the" *one yet to come and rule for a short space?*"

1. Justinian 554 -586 A.D. Prophetic 1ˢᵗ Head 4ᵗʰ Horn Justinian has sometimes been known as the "last Roman" in mid-20ᵗʰ century historiography. This ambition was expressed by the partial recovery of the territories of the defunct Western Roman Empire. (1ˢᵗ Resurrection of Roman Empire)

2. Charlemagne 800-924 A.D. Prophetic 2ⁿᵈ Head 5ᵗʰ Horn He even minted coins with the inscription, *"Empire Restored"* He was crowned by the Pope while kneeling. Many do not realize that Charlemagne was a German. (2ⁿᵈ Resurrection of Roman Empire)

3. Otto the Great 962-1250 A.D. Prophetic 3ʳᵈ Head 6ᵗʰ Horn These empires were all dominated by German Emperors.

Crowned at Aachen Otto's coronation was of Roman origin. Known also as the East Frankish kingdom, or Germany. It emerged as the strongest power in Europe during this time. Otto was an ardent friend of the Roman Catholic Church. This "empire of the west" continued for almost 800 years in a loose Italo-German phase. Eventually a struggle between German Emperors and the Popes ended with an agreement in1122A.D. that caused the emperor to relinquish the right of spiritual investiture to the Pope. (3ʳᵈ Resurrection of Roman Empire)

NOTE: *Frederick Barbarossa a German emperor in 1157 A.D. was the first to use the phrase, Holy Roman Empire. He was attempting to restore and perpetuate the ancient Roman Empire.*

---

[66] *Daniel 7:7-8*

(7) After this I saw in the night visions, and behold a fourth beast, dreadful and terrible, and strong exceedingly; and it had great iron teeth: it devoured and brake in pieces, and stamped the residue with the feet of it: and it was diverse from all the beasts that were before it; and it had ten horns.

(8) I considered the horns, and, behold, **there came up among them another little horn,** <u>before whom there were three of the first horns plucked up by the roots</u>*: and, behold,* <u>in this horn were eyes like the eyes of man, and a mouth speaking great things.</u> *(The Papacy)*

4. Charles V 1273-1806 A.D. Prophetic 4th Head 7th Horn This was when the Eastern Empire of Rome ended. Some of it transferred to Imperial Russia under Ivan III. His marriage to Zoe by the Pope was an attempt to bring the Russians into the Roman Church. (4th Resurrection of the Roman Empire)

NOTE: *It is during the 12th and 13th centuries when **German powers** were being dismantled, the **Popes** of that time accumulated titles, ranks, offices, and duties of the Emperor's and the Empire.*

What is known as the Holy Roman Empire, a political entity in western Europe from 800 to 1806 A.D.

The title Holy Roman Empire was adopted in the 13th century. Its principal area was always the German states. The Holy Roman Empire was an attempt to revive the Western Roman Empire which deteriorated during the 5th and 6th centuries being replaced by independent kingdoms ruled by German nobles.

(Are you seeing an obvious connection here between Roman Church and German Rulers?)

5. Napoleon Bonaparte 1804-1814 A.D. Prophetic 5th Head 8th Horn

Napoleon allied with the Hapsburgs to recreate the Holy Roman Empire. The Revolution of 1789 -1814 was considered as the Roman Republic and the Holy Roman Empire. He followed the tradition of the emperor-Pope tensions over the centuries by claiming himself as the Emperor of the Roman system and the power of the Popes behind the Emperor's throne. Napoleon was a manipulator in truth, during the crowning ceremony, he took the crown from the Pope crowned himself Emperor and then in 1804 proclaimed himself King of Italy.

He was a narcissist that was out of control, arresting Pope Pius VII, annexed the Papal states, plundered their churches, and erected a pagan edifice outside St. Peter's.

[67] **Note:** *This Emperor's desire to be worshipped as a god will play out again in the last days scenario of the Beast and False Prophet! The latter day 10 Kings of the Beast Power will hate the False Prophet and destroy him and the church.*

Napoleon's ambitions caused Francis II to abolish the Holy Roman Empire to keep Napoleon from taking possession of it. Francis II created the Austro-Hungarian Empire. It became known as the **"Secret Holy Roman Empire."**

This covert Empire was destroyed by the Anglo-Saxon powers in **1918**. It is no coincidence that the **Holy Roman Empire** disappears during the years of the rise of **Britain** and **America,** the very nations that smashed the attempts at world conquest in WWI and WWII.

(Latter day blessings from Jacob coming to pass as Britain and America take the world in leadership and dominance)

It is obvious that when Britain and America rise to national power from WWI and WWII that the conquest for world domination is put to rest.

The Church of Rome Briefly Separates from the Beast

Napoleon's reign was a Holy Roman Empire in spirit. Though he was not legally considered the Emperor of the Church he still fulfills the office of leader in the Western half of the Empire. The Empire was split into two halves. The Western half was a confederation of France and Germans. In the East, this half was the Austro-Hungarian Empire or as some historians label it; *"The Secret Holy Roman Empire."* So, the beast continued in the East even when Napoleon fell in the West.

The demised Western Empire was then replaced with the **German Confederation** in an act of the **Congress of Vienna, June 8, 1815.**

The **"Secret Holy Roman Empire"** was absorbed into the German **Second Reich** by **1866** until it was crushed by the Brits and Americans of

---

67   Rev 13:17-18

(17) And that no man might buy or sell, save he that had the mark, or the name of the beast, or the number of his name.

(18) Here is wisdom. Let him that hath understanding count the number of the beast: for it is the number of a man; and his number is Six hundred threescore and six.

WWI in 1918. Therefore, I label it as the **6th Head of the Seven Headed Beast Power.**

6. The German Second Reich 1871 – 1918 "one is" Prophetic 6th Head 9th Horn This conquest of the Germans in WWI ended the (6th resurrection of the Holy Roman Empire.)

From this time forward the Holy Roman Empire was starting to recreate a Christian Europe.

NOTE: *"It was in 1913 that the Federal Reserve and Internal Revenue Service were established to monitor and control interest rates and taxes in America. Baby step toward New World Order economically."*

7. The German Third Reich 1939 – 1945 "one is yet to come" Prophetic 7th Head 10th Horn (7th resurrection of the Empire)

Hitler's basic political plans for Europe were patterned after Napoleon. However, Hitler upon visiting Napoleon's tomb, swore he would not make the mistakes Napoleon made.

Although Hitler was a non-Catholic neo-pagan, he like Napoleon saw Catholics as a stabilizing power for his Reich.

I choose the German 3rd Reich for the 7th Head of the Beast. The atrocities committed during WWII by the Germans are horrible and mirror the actions of their ancestors the Assyrians. Many during the forty's thought Hitler was the predicted anti-Christ. His atrocities against the Jews are horrific in nature just as the Assyrians performed in the early centuries. The Assyrians are the ancestors of the Germans. (*Ethnically speaking*)

Their instinct is to lay low for years and then suddenly rise to power to conquer and reinstate their mission to be the "master race" and rule the world.

God used America and Briton to stop this madness by ending it in WWII.

However, look at Germany today; reunited, strong, and quietly waiting for America to fall economically.

Chart overview of Beast Empires from History

Revelation 17:7

*(7) And the angel said unto me, Wherefore didst thou marvel? I will tell thee the mystery of the woman, and **of the beast that carries her, which hath the seven heads and ten horns.***

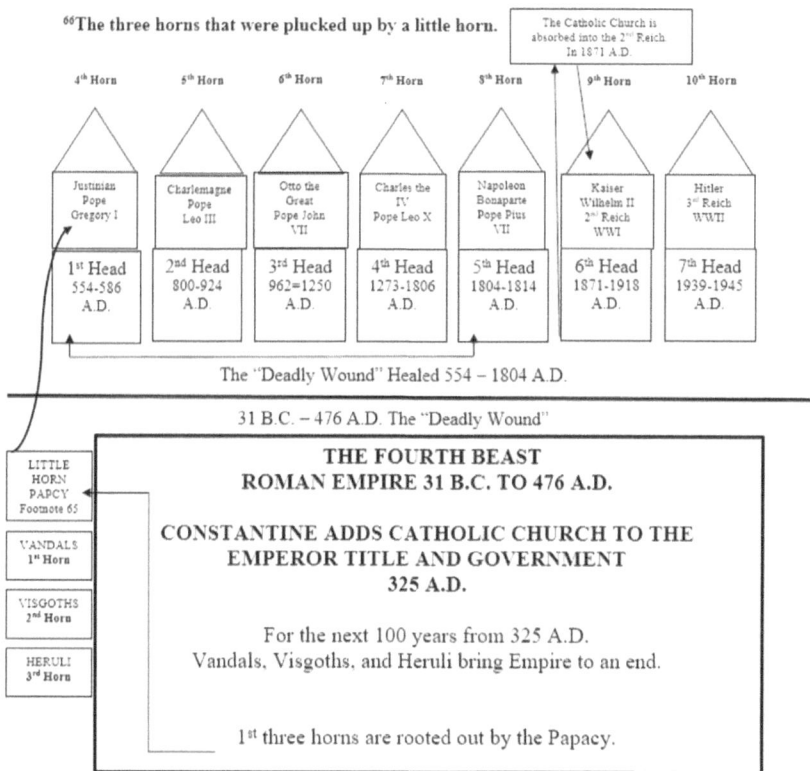

Before we continue, it is important to understand the Science of genetic memories and the German *"mind-set."* This is important in making my case for the coming Beast Power in charge of the New World Order being a German dominate power.

Scientific Proof of Behavioral Instincts Stimulated

I have compared the ancestral physic link between ancient races of people and modern instincts; though speculation on my part, consider what science says about the collective unconscious mind: It is ***"an invisible membrane which unites nations and causes them to act in unison"*** says a scientist when discussing the functions of memory in humans. Scientist have proved the difficulty in overwriting established neuro-circuits, in the biology of the human brain, is **the reason for phobias** that are difficult to cure. After treatment that appears successful, fearful memories lurk deep within the brain.

He goes on to say, *"I have witnessed the reactivation of phobia in an individual when they suddenly came under stress. The stress caused the neuropath of terrifying memories come to life once again, causing them to react in an unpredictable manner. This happened after months of therapy to overcome the phobia."*

Scientists offer three aspects to consider about human behavior pattern:

- One, a collective mind the product of *"mental telepathy"* which link it with consecutive generations of ethnicity.
- Two, a collective unconscious mind is inherited from generations, and **does not develop individually on its own**. It is an unconscious mind that mirrors a world of pure archetypes stored in our mind all our life. ***Neuropathways*** from them, suddenly stimulated, become a pattern of our personality and behavior. This is true of all humans. We share some common memories and experiences which jointly owned racial treasures are stored in our collective unconscious mental biology. (*Some call it a "rallying point" within the person*)
- Three, inherited unconscious memory is an *"instinct"* causing humans to react nationally in the aftermath of crisis. The existence of a racial memory or *"instinct"* is not absorbed by one generation and then remembered by the next generations but, traumatic and repetitious impressions experienced by earlier generations can

biologically become permanent <u>unconscious aid to the mind, or *"instinct"* carried on through bloodlines. This instinctive behavior can be a predicted response akin to specific nationalities.</u>

Simply put, it is like *"he's a hothead"* or *"she's always going to blush at certain questions."* Some say, *"red heads have a temper!"* or *"the Scottish are a stingy people,"* or the *"Irish are stubborn."*

I said all this to make this point about *"Instinctive Behavior":* Especially in a national pride sense.

This should help you to understand why there have been wars and conflicts among nations for 4,000 years. Inherent proclivities of violence exist in some ethnic groups of people. Therefore, God chose the nation of Israel to spread His will among the nations down through history. (*Emphasis mine*)

It takes the Holy Spirit of God in a person to overcome such inherited behavioral traits. This is why a personal relationship with Jesus Christ is important to all people who expect to survive the New World Order and Armageddon.

THE GERMAN MIND-SET

I have determined that **Germans**, for example, operate in <u>predictable cycles of peace and war</u>. At this present time, they are in the ***pacifist phase*** of their cycle. Example: They reflect no visible manifestation of violence toward other nations. In fact, they recently took in Syrian refugees when other countries would not. Inherit characteristics of a people **do not change over the centuries**. They might modify and periodically restrain, but they are the same deep down inside.

One of their famous writers says it for them, ***"We Germans were leading the people of Europe, we were the most warlike people ever to have existed on earth."*** Wolfgang Menzel said this**, he lived 1799-1873**. An overview of their history engaging wars validates my suspicions. Following are 11 of many German engagements of war.

1. Early tribal wars
2. Early medieval wars
3. Later medieval wars

4. The Thirty Years war
5. The wars of Fredrick the Great
6. The Revolutionary and Napoleonic wars
7. The Danish wars
8. The Austro-Prussian war
9. The Franco-German war
10. World War One
11. World War Two

It is no wonder the modern Germans have deleted their ancestors from their history and denied the events of WWII. Do you see a pattern of behavior in ancient **Assyrians** that is in the **Germans** down through history?

Do you recall what nationality was hired by the Romans to fight their wars? This was because the Romans noticed The German's overriding character, it is the cruel, aggressive, warlike nature of the Germans. For centuries, the Roman army consisted of foreigners, chiefly Germans. They have always been noted for their warlike attributes. The ancient Roman historian, **Tacitus,** has very much to say about the Germans as he writes during the latter half of the first century A.D. Following are his observations.

- The Germans worshipped the god Tuisto.
- Their youths sought out other tribes who were at war if their own tribe was stagnating under a protracted peace.
- They had no taste for peace.
- They loved indolence but hated peace. They taught Rome the severest lessons.
- The Germans were the fiercest soldiers in the Roman army.
- They mercilessly tortured their Roman prisoners.
- Surpassed all nations in arms and in loyalty.
- Had a passion for deciding all issues by the sword.

Now recall how much German domination is responsible for the biblical prophecy of *"healing of the deadly wound"* inflicted on the Fourth Beast Rome; then reviving it into the Holy Roman Empire of sorts up until

1918 A.D.? I recall two *world wars* started by Germany. Where is Russia in all this history? I do not see any end time Russia as the *"beast power."*

Throughout the history of the bible, God has used **Assyrian Kings** and armies to punish His people. God has prophesies thru Daniel of kingdoms of mankind that will rise and fall through history. Why wouldn't God use the descendants of the Assyrians to bring people once again into humility and submission? There is a relationship between Germans and Catholic.

One only must watch the American History Channel to get a picture of this Beast/False Prophet relationship. After WWII when Nazi criminals from the war were being sought for prosecution; many were found in France, hiding within and under the protection of the Catholic Bishops. As far away as Brazil and countries in South America these Nazi War Lords were found living under the protection of the Catholic Bishops. There is factual evidence of this long-standing relationship between the **Germans** and **Catholic Church** down through history.

Even though the descendants of Araxphad (America/Britain) crushed Hitler's attempts at world domination, it does not mean it is not still alive in the hearts of Germans.

It manifested twice, once in WWI and again in WWII. I have demonstrated it down through history to be an ongoing relationship between power and religion to rule the world and become the "Master Race" of humanity to keep order in the world.

Twice the Germans have been defeated in this attempt. The next time, the third and final war will end up in Armageddon with Christ putting an end to their conquest.

A nation's collective mind and character, its actions, and thoughts, has been shaped by generations of experience and reactions to various stimuli and kept within the racial memory of nations. <u>Down through history, behavioral patterns appear which become deeply ingrained due to repetitive activities.</u> These behavior patterns carry through generations by the collective biological genes and subconsciousness of the nation. <u>This becomes the proclivity of a nation or its national character if aroused.</u>

THE REICH CONCEPT

<u>Satan's Counterfeit of the 1,000 Years Reign of Jesus Christ</u>

- ➤ This philosophy began in **962-1806 A.D.** Time period for the **1ˢᵗ Reich**.
- ➤ The **2ⁿᵈ Reich** began in **1871-1918 A.D.** with the ending of WWI.
- ➤ The **3ʳᵈ Reich** began in **1934** with Adolf Hitler's movement and ended in 1945 with the end of WWII.

The German Reich concept promotes that the **German race** is the peace-giver of the world—that it is a joint **Christian/Roman concept** that needs to be in place for the regency of the Kingdom of God on earth. Many of their writings state that the task of the Empire is to be God's protagonist on earth, to fulfill God's will on earth while protecting Christianity and the church. Their goal is to preserve the righteousness of God and the divine order of the universe on earth. *(It is their version of what Christ will establish on earth)*

This Empire of physical men on earth is the transitory reflection of the eternal City of God *(not unlike what Assur, Nimrod, and Semiramis tried to do with Nineveh and the Tower of Babel)*. They claim God creates the **Holy Roman Empire for Christianity** to expand over the entire earth. **These German scholars and political elite still operate in spirit.** Frederick William IV of Germany dreams of a revived Holy Roman Empire to replace the German Confederation. *(This is Satan's plan from the day after the flood of Noah's time)*

The Holy Roman Empire seeks to recreate **a united Christian Europe** in similitude to the last years of the Roman Empire. *(Wolf in Sheep's clothing)* They secretly advocate a **European Union**. They call it holy **because of the supremacy of the Pope in ecclesiastical affairs**. The Pope is religious ruler, and the German Emperors are the secular arm and defender of the Catholic Church.

<u>Has anyone noticed how the Holy Roman Empire disappears during the years of the rise of Britain and America?</u> America, the icon of freedom and Democracy. These two nations smash attempts at world conquest led

by Germany and the axis powers in World Wars I and II. These wars are the second and third attempts at a Reich concept fostered by Germans. Even though the Holy Roman Empire disappears, the **Vatican is now an isolated empire of power influencing the world.**

Notice this recent article about the Pope advocating more "global authority."

UPDATE MARCH 6, 2019

Speaking with Ecuador's "El Universe" newspaper, the Pope said that the United Nations doesn't have enough power and must be granted full governmental control "for the good of humanity."

But what is raising eyebrows is the Pope's call for a new global political authority. *Here is more from the Guardian:*

Pope Francis will this week call for changes in lifestyles and energy consumption to avert the "unprecedented destruction of the ecosystem" before the end of this century, according to a leaked draft of a papal encyclical. In a document released by an Italian magazine on Monday, the pontiff will warn that failure to act would have "grave consequences for all of us."

Francis also called for a new global political authority tasked with "tackling … the reduction of pollution and the development of poor countries and regions." ***His appeal echoed that of his predecessor, pope Benedict XVI,*** *who in a 2009 encyclical proposed a kind of super-UN to deal with the world's economic problems and injustices.*

The word "globalization" means exactly what it says. It is the process of transitioning the world into a global government. Religious leaders are playing their part in this great deception.

David Rockefeller famously said that a "global crisis" would have to occur before the people of the world would be willing to accept a **New World Order.** *When the world economy suffered a dramatic crash in 2008,* **world leaders again proclaimed the need for a New World Order with global financial control.**

As demonstrated by **Pope Francis***, climate change and the global warming hoax is now the global elite's preferred method of scaremongering, as they attempt to shepherd humanity closer to unified totalitarian rule.*

Disturbingly, world religious leaders are also beginning to come together as one to preach from the same hymn sheet, **instructing their sheep to accept the components of the New World Order's one world government.**

In case you missed it, world leaders from a diverse collection of religious communities called for world unity in a video message released last week.

The call for a world government, led by Pope Francis, Ayatollah Al-Milani, the Dalai Lama and Rabbi Abraham Skorka, *is seen as a major step on the road to the* **New World Order** *that was prophesied over 2,000 years ago.*

The world religious leaders came together on June 14 to make a joint statement through a video calling on people to embrace ideas of friendship and unity, and to overcome negativity and division in society.

The call for global government by Pope Francis *and other wealthy elitists has nothing to do with lifting impoverished nations or "saving humanity." Such a government would instead guarantee global surveillance, global wealth inequality and a world run by the exact corrupt interests currently consolidating wealth and power worldwide.*

The New World Order is a real concept:

This is another steppingstone toward the New World Order of men! They openly advocate this concept. This world dominance will involve the currency of the world being changed from the American dollar to the "Deutsch mark" or Euro dollar of the United States Common Market of Europe!

[68]Wait and see: Germany will rise again to be the power over the United States of Europe and will demand other nations join or be shut out. What will America do? Britain already wants out of the common market.

Events Leading to A New World Order

The idea and aspiration of a world government order has been in the minds of mankind since the dawn of history. Bronze Age Egyptian Kings aimed to rule "All That the Sun Encircles", Mesopotamian Kings "All from the Sunrise to the Sunset", and ancient Chinese and Japanese Emperors "All under Heaven". These four civilizations developed impressive cultures of Great Unity, or Da Yitong as the Chinese put it. In 113 BC, the Han Dynasty in China erected an Altar of the Great Unity.

World government or global government is the nation of a common political authority for all of humanity. It is a global government and a

---

[68]   *Revelation 13:16-17*

   (16) And he causes all, both small and great, rich and poor, free and bond, to receive a mark in their right hand, or in their foreheads:
   (17) And that no man might buy or sell, save he that had the mark, or the name of the beast, or the number of his name.

single state that exercises authority over the entire Earth. Such a government could come into existence either through violent and compulsory world domination or through peaceful and voluntary *"supranational union."*

I offer the following information to support my reasoning for the beast power of the end times to be **a German military force** dominating the events of the Middle East. Please remember all we have covered thus far about the ancestors and active association of Germany down through history and their ties to wars and the Catholic Religion.

A supranational union is a type of multinational political union where negotiated power is delegated to an authority by governments of member states. The concept of supranational union is sometimes used to describe the European Union (EU), as a new type of political entity. The EU is the only entity which provides for international popular elections, going beyond the level of political integration normally afforded by international treaty. The term *"supranational"* is sometimes used in a loose, undefined sense in other contexts, sometimes as a substitute for international, transnational, or global. Another method of decision-making in international organizations is intergovernmentalism, in which state governments play a more prominent role.

There has not been a worldwide ruling government since the last days of Napoleon in 1806 A.D. Now, we have the **United Nations**. It is limited to a mostly advisory role. Its stated purpose is to promote co-operation between existing national government membership, rather than exert authority over them.

The **European Union** of today is somewhere between **Federalism**, an arrangement of government like the United States of America, and a confederation or a league of nations as a union of sovereign states. They are united for purposes of common action often in relation to other states.

The European Economic Community was described by its founder Robert Schuman as midway between confederacies which recognizes the complete independence of States in an association and federalism which seeks to fuse them in a super-state. The EU has supranational competences, but it possesses these competences only to the extent that they are conferred on it by its member states. This is called Kompetenz-Kompetenz; or competence-competence, is a jurisprudential doctrine whereby a legal body, such as a court or arbitral tribunal, may have competence, or jurisdiction, to rule as to the extent of its own competence on an issue before it. The concept arose in the Federal Constitutional Court of Germany.

The Europe Declaration, also known as the Charter of the Community, was a joint statement issued by the Foreign Ministers of West Germany, France, Italy, the Netherlands, Belgium, and Luxembourg in 1951. It reads as follows:

> *"By the signature of this Treaty, the involved parties give proof of their determination to create the first supranational institution and that thus they are laying the true foundation of an organized Europe. This Europe is still open to all European countries that have freedom of choice. We profoundly hope that other countries will join us in our common endeavor."*

It was made to recall future generations to their historic duty of uniting Europe based on liberty and democracy under the rule of law. Thus, they viewed the creation of a wider and deeper Europe as intimately bound to the healthy development of the supranational or Community system.

Signature of the Treaty of Rome

A conference led to the signature, on 25 March 1957, of the Treaty establishing the European Economic Community and the Euratom Treaty at the Palazzo Dei Conservatory on Capitoline Hill in Rome.

In March 2007, the BBC's Today radio program reported that delays in printing the treaty meant that the document signed by the European leaders as the Treaty of Rome consisted of blank pages between its frontispiece and page for the signatures.

The Treaty of Rome, the original full name of which was the Treaty establishing the European Economic Community has been amended by successive treaties significantly changing its content. The 1992 Treaty of Maastricht established the European Union, the EEC becoming one of its three pillars, the European Community. Hence, the treaty was renamed the Treaty establishing the European Community (TEC).

When the Treaty of Lisbon came into force in 2009, the pillar system was abandoned; hence, the EC ceased to exist as a legal entity separate from the EU. This led to the treaty being amended and renamed as the Treaty on the Functioning of the European Union (TFEU).

In March 2011, the European Council adopted a decision to amend the Treaty by adding a new paragraph to Article 136. The additional paragraph, which enables the establishment of a financial stability mechanism for the Eurozone, runs as follows:

> "The Member States whose currency is the euro may set up a stability mechanism to be activated if indispensable to safeguard the stability of the euro area. The granting of any required financial aid under the mechanism will be made subject to strict conditionality."

What does all this mean? It simply ties the ideals of a United Europe that will someday become the powerful, world dominating, force to bring a New World Order of peace. There will eventually be a brief time of peace in the Middle East. This will allow the Jews to build a third Temple for their religious order. It will be a smaller version than the first two from history. I sight the following scripture as speculation on size of this temple.

Revelation 11:1-2

(1) *And there was given me a reed like unto a rod: and the angel stood, saying, Rise, and measure the temple of God, and the altar, and them that worship therein.*

(2) **But the court, which is without the temple leave out**, and **measure it not**; *for it is given unto the Gentiles: and the holy city shall they tread under foot forty and two months.*

There is not enough space for the outer court today, this is because of the Islamic Mosque or Dome of the Rock already on the temple site. They will build between the "Wailing Wall" and the Dome of the Rock. Part of the peace agreement would be to leave the Muslim Dome of the Rock undisturbed. (*speculation*)

Next, after a pseudo peace agreement is secured between Israel and Palestine, the Jews will begin work on the third Temple in Jerusalem.

These people are passionate about the third Temple. Following is a quote from Hillel the 3rd from the first century:

Hillel the third ended his assessment of how Jews will always feel about their religion, temple, and land in his sixth letter to the Jews in captivity.

"Though we may be thousands of miles away, and be sold into bondage, and bound in chains, yet we will not, we cannot, forget our land, our religion, and our God. He is the God of Abraham, and still is merciful, and will remember His promises and keep His covenant made with our fathers."

THE TEMPLE MOUNT FAITHFUL

About 24 years ago, the founder of this organization, **Gershon Solomon,** is marching to the ancient temple with a symbolic Cornerstone to be set in place for the **3rd Temple**! His mission is interrupted by a staged riot by the Palestinian Arabs. People are killed there, and Gershon Solomon is about a kilometer away from the sight. He abandons the march and goes to the **wailing wall** where he witnesses thousands of stones hailing down upon the worshippers! In the interview from a short while after that event, Solomon said the attack was not a result of their mission to lay a symbolic Cornerstone. The Israeli military previously informed the Palestinian Arabs that the march will not involve their Mosque or Dome of the Rock area. The Palestinians rioted anyway.

This is the passion of the **Temple Mount Faithful** over 24 years ago, and it has not diminished in zealous passion to this day, in building a Temple! Building this temple is in their heart and soul! There will be a third temple for the Jews before Christ returns.

Following is an excerpt from the Temple Mount Foundation in Jerusalem:

*****Temple Mount Faithful** to President Donald Trump: "Declare, Call, and Stand with Israel to Build the Third Temple in Jerusalem Like King Cyrus of Persia Did in 536 BC." "Call the Pope to Return the Temple Menorah and Articles to Jerusalem to Be Used by Israel in the **Third Holy Temple**, soon to Be Built, Like **King Cyrus***

Did When He Returned the Temple Menorah and Articles from Babylon to Be Used in the Second Temple."

The Temple Mount and Land of Israel Faithful Movement blesses President Donald Trump upon his election as the next president to lead the United States of America. Today we are blessing President Donald Trump with an ancient Jewish blessing: "Blessed are You our LORD, King of Kings, for sharing His honor with human beings".

"Many in Israel think and believe that the election of President Donald Trump was not an accident, but rather an important part of end-time events that we are now experiencing during this significant era of modern history. President Trump appeared suddenly from nowhere. He never was an active member or an official in any of the political parties in the United States. He came with a completely different vision from all other candidates in the recent elections and especially different from the previous president that served before him. His vision for America is to return to the vision of the founding fathers of America, a vision based and adopted from the biblical mandate laid out by the prophets of Israel.

More than this, President Donald Trump was elected by the American people with great excitement and expectation, especially concerning his vision and policy toward the greatest ally of the United States, Israel. Allow us to say at this point, considering the fact that we are living during a very "rational and intellectual era in history" when so many people and nations have rejected any authentic spiritual understanding and have put God in the corner of their lives and have forgotten that there is only One Who leads mankind: It is only God, our Creator, who leads the universe. It is God Who caused this "revolutionary" choice, as it looks, in the United States that led to the election of Donald Trump. Regarding all the unusual circumstances, we want to say that the election of President Donald Trump was a godly event. Despite that Donald Trump did not say so, it was only God Who directed him to carry such a vision of returning to the roots of America's foundation which were based on the biblical vision. He knew very clearly that this was the desire of the American people, and he knew to put it during his vision for America and to pronounce it so openly and clearly with no fear. For decades, this has been the vision of the Bible Belt of America and now it has started to become a major reality in the life of the United States.

Indeed, it is not an accident that America has stood with Israel for such a long time. However, the American presidents before President Trump so often did not understand that the mission of America regarding Israel cannot be fulfilled without truly recognizing the godly mission of Israel among the nations. President Obama made a profound mistake by not recognizing Jerusalem as the eternal capital of the God and people of Israel and by not understanding that all the Land of Israel was given by God only to His people Israel for an eternal purpose. Instead of this, he initiated and supported anti-godly pressure on Israel to divide her Land and to establish an anti-godly so-called "Palestinian" state during the Holy Land of Israel. President Donald Trump understands what former presidents did not understand and that is the genuine desire of the American people to stand side-by-side with Israel.

The Temple Mount and Land of Israel Faithful Movement is calling President Trump to fulfill completely all his promises to Israel. He is also called to fulfill the expectation of the God and people of Israel to immediately move with no delay the American embassy to Jerusalem. This is a fundamental need for America. In doing this, President Trump will be tested by God, history, and the American people. We are calling him not to fear whatever opposition that will try to pressure him to change any of his promises, especially regarding Jerusalem and his new policy towards Israel. He should know that God is with him if he trusts God and not any human powers and if he fulfills his promises and his new policy towards Israel.

The Temple Mount and the Land of Israel Faithful Movement is calling President Donald Trump to stand with Israel in her main mission to build the Third Holy Temple on the Holy Temple Mount in Jerusalem and to fulfill the call of the God of Israel to do it in the lifetime of our generation with no delay. It will be the greatest day for all humanity when Israel will invite the God of Israel and the universe to dwell in His Holy House in Jerusalem during the life of His people Israel and the entire world.

When the vision of God of thousands of years that always pointed to our end-time generation is fulfilled, it will open a new and unique age that never was before, an age of true worldwide peace when God will reign amid His capital in Jerusalem and bless all His creation.

As you can see, we are experiencing a special time in the history of humanity and throughout the world that never occurred before. This is the age that the prophets of Israel referred to as the "end-times." God is preparing His people

Israel and even the entire world for the climax of this time: the building of the Third Holy Temple in Jerusalem from where the God of Israel will reign over the entire world and all mankind. Time is short and the Faithful Movement is called to be ready.

The Temple Mount and Land of Israel Faithful Movement is working intensively to answer the challenges of this special time. The Faithful Movement is now working day and night to fulfill her two main goals: First, is to answer the call of God to rebuild the Holy Temple in Jerusalem with no delay, to be a "House of Prayer for all nations" (Isaiah 56:7). Second, is to answer the call of God to Israel to be ready to fulfill her mission: "...to be a holy nation, a kingdom of priests and a light to the nations" (Exodus 19:5,6; Isaiah 42:6; 49:6). We are now called to double our efforts to push forward the fulfillment of God's call to rebuild the Holy Temple in Jerusalem. We cannot even imagine how it will be fulfilled without your encouragement, standing with the Faithful Movement and financial help. Together with the God of Israel and all of you, we can do it, and we shall do it, God willing!

On this occasion, we want to thank our friends and brothers so very much and sisters who already help us in fulfilling our holy work. Everyone is called to help the Faithful Movement to bring to pass her major historical mission and to answer the call of the God of Israel and to be blessed by Him in actively having an important part in this greatest cause ever:"

This is an article to remember. The Jews are serious about the **third Temple**. I am amazed they even invite the Pope to give up the **Temple Menorah**. They have included scriptures to support their zeal for peace and a temple.

Here is another event in 2017 that the Jews feel is significant to prophecy.

An Exciting Prophetic Event – Fulfillment of End Time Prophecy and Another Step Towards the Soon Building of the Third Holy Temple

"On the 29th of June 2017, a Jewish wedding took place on the Holy Temple Mount in Jerusalem. This marked another major step of Israel and the Faithful Movement towards the soon building of the Third Holy Temple in the lifetime of our generation. The wedding was done secretly because the

Israeli authorities continue to fear Arab, Islamic, and international reaction if any Jewish activities are conducted on the Holy Temple Mount. The Faithful Movement calls the Israeli authorities, again and again, not to fear any human reaction but rather to trust only the God of Israel. The Movement prays and strengthens her activities that this day will soon come."

Because the year of Jubilee is 2017, the Jews are excited about building this third Temple. Following is an excerpt from an article from the Temple Mount Foundation:

A Major Step in the Campaign to Build the Third Holy Temple in 2017: An Urgent Call to the Government of Israel: Worship and Prayer at the "Kotel", Which Symbolizes Destruction and Exile, Is Over! It Is Time to Worship and Pray Only at the Proper Place: on the Holy Temple Mount in Jerusalem!

The Temple Mount and Land of Israel Faithful Movement is urgently calling the government of Israel to take brave historical Jubilee steps to mark the 50th anniversary of the 1967 liberation of the Holy Temple Mount and biblical Jerusalem:

- *Step one, move all prayer and worship from the Western Wall ("Kotel"), which symbolizes destruction and exile and start prayer and worship at the only proper place, the Holy Temple Mount.*
- *Step two, at once start rebuilding the Holy Temple on God's Holy Hill, on the Holy Temple Mount in Jerusalem!*

Israel is preparing to welcome and celebrate the exciting 50th anniversary year of Jubilee of the godly liberation of the Holy Temple Mount, biblical Jerusalem, and the biblical areas of Judea, Samaria, Gaza, the Golan Heights, and the Sinai after hundreds of years of foreign Islamic occupation of the most holy places of the Jewish people.

It is the time for these two important steps to be taken during this commemorative Jubilee year of the major redemption that is taking place in Israel as the beginning of world-wide redemption. These crucial steps will stop the shameful situation of the people of God praying at the Kotel, outside of the Holy Temple Mount, while the enemy of the God and people of Israel continue to abominate and desecrate the Name of the God of Israel and calls from the Holy Mountain to kill Jews and to destroy Israel. The God of Israel is mourning in heaven about this unbelievable situation when this abomination occurs under Israeli independence and sovereignty. This unspeakable situation never happened throughout the history of Israel. Israel should at once take steps to halt the offensive situation on the Holy Temple Mount and immediately answer the call of God to His people.

If this abominable status on the Holy Temple Mount continues and the government of Israel does not stop it because of pressure and threats from worldwide foreign powers and because of putting its trust in human strategies, there will never be peace in the Middle East and in the entire world.

This is "in-line" with events that will precede the New World Order; however, this peace and tranquility they hope for will be short lived, according to the prophesies of the bible.

Back to 1946 and an overlooked step toward New World Order

Next, I will introduce you to a post WWII speech that most people don't even know about. This happened in 1946 just after WWII while Britain, America, and Russia were deciding how to handle the conquered Germany.

POST WWII ATTEMPT TO GET CONTROL OF NATIONS

We have seen how the **Holy Roman Empire** disappears during the years of the rise of Britain and America. America, the icon of freedom and Democracy. These two nations smashed attempts at world conquest led by Germany and the axis powers in World Wars I and II. Even though the Holy Roman Empire disappears, the **Vatican is now an isolated empire of power. The Catholic Church** made a case, for their influence as the worldwide "*moral compass*" in late 1945, during the dividing of conquered Germany between the Allied Forces that won WWII. They expressed the need for a world religion at that time to direct the nations.

Most people have forgotten the conferences held in San Francisco, California, in the late 1945 decline of World War II. Germany was soon being defeated, and the three main allies—the **United States**, **Russia**, and

Great Britain—engaged in a quest to prevent another Worldwide War from happening again. The **League of Nations** was the precursor to the forming of the United Nations in 1946. The **San Francisco Conference** is significant to this timeline because of its intended purposes and the warning from the leaders of the Catholic Church that without their oversight, the United Nations would eventually fail! They were once again trying to revive that system of religion governing over the nations of the world.

During the conference of 1945 there was a **Solemn Pontifical Mass** staged by the **Roman Catholic Church**. In an Auditorium that seated 10,000, every seat was filled. Most people aren't even aware of this event.

After much ritual and such, a sermon was given by **Duane G. Hunt**, radio spokesman for the church. *(From 1927 to 1949, Hunt was the weekly speaker on NBC's Catholic Hour, a radio program on which he discussed Catholic doctrine.)* Seated right in front of him were 300 delegates of the conference from Europe and South America. The Catholic hierarchy was aware of the bickering and strife among the nations' delegates, even though the world leaders proclaimed otherwise. The Catholic service offered the world leaders the world's last hope for peace. They characterized their offer as the **Last Straw** for the eventual drowning nations of the conference to grab, when they shall later see their world organization sinking into failure and oblivion. Without divine help, the newly formed United Nations structure was doomed to collapse. That divine help was offered by the Roman Catholic Church. Without the guidance and supervision of authority of the Church they were laboring in vain, is what was said.

This sermon was a *"**physiological seed**"* destined to unite under **Catholicism a Europe** that would resurrect the **Holy Roman Empire** once again. Their whole platform was built on men left to themselves, allowing their baser inclinations unrestrained, with selfishness given free reign. There could be no peace or order in the world. Hunt said that government derived its civil authority from God, and **the Catholic Church was God's government over nations**. The Catholic interpretation is that **God rules on earth through the Papacy and the Roman Catholic Church**. Whatever the Pope binds on earth is bound in heaven. **The Pope is the Vicar of Christ. He is supposed to be in authority over all kings and governments.**

This conference was over 70 years ago, and the United Nations is still struggling to keep peace worldwide. The Catholic Church has remained satisfied with their converts all over the world. The various Popes are still influential in some nations of the world. This concept of One World Government is still in the hearts and minds of the Europeans today. Every so often a step forward in show of religious influence and power comes out of the Papacy.

Wow! This makes what we are learning from this book especially important to our future!

I will simply say, they are a force to deal with on the world scene, especially in the coming events of the future. They are like **their own sovereign nation**, untouchable by other nations. [69]However, their history tells me to consider them for participation with **the 8th Beast that is of the 7th mentioned in biblical prophecy** for the time of Armageddon.

There are a lot of events that must happen before this 8th Edition of the Beast comes on the scene. I have laid a lot of background information that points directly to the Germans and the Catholic Pope. I believe they will be the leaders of the coming Beast Power and New World Order! Of course, we will have to wait and see. History repeats itself so many times. Even many of the prophesies in the Bible are "Dual" with interpretation, a former, and a latter fulfillment.

Once this New World Order is in place the prophesies of Revelation and other scriptures will come into focus. Especially Revelation. Therefore, I believe a detailed enhancement of the book of Revelation is necessary to prove my suspicions for the "players" in the coming New World Order.

I will leave this chapter with an overview of the Fourth Beast from start to finish for a reference to help us see the picture of history and probable future.

---

[69] *Matthew 24:4-5*

(4) And Jesus answered and said unto them, Take heed that no man deceive you. (5) For many shall come in my name, saying, I am Christ; and shall deceive many.
2Thessalonians 2:1-4
(1) Now we beseech you, brethren, by the coming of our Lord Jesus Christ, and by our gathering together unto him, (2) That ye be not soon shaken in mind, or be troubled, neither by spirit, nor by word, nor by letter as from us, as that the day of Christ is at hand. (3) Let no man deceive you by any means: for that day shall not come, except there come a falling away first, and that man of sin be revealed, the son of perdition; (4) Who opposes and exalts himself above all that is called God, or that is worshipped; so that he as God sits in the temple of God, shewing himself that he is God.

> *I see <u>the Beast who, was, is not, and yet is; the eighth who is of the seventh</u> to be a Military Force of the United States of Europe with ten Prime Ministers or Kings, ruled and enforced by a Germany in harmony with the Catholic Church being the spiritual peacemaker for the world. This will be an alliance between the Beast and the False Prophet for 3.5 years before the coming Great Tribulation that will be for the last 3.5 years completing the 70 Weeks Prophecy of Daniel Chapter Nine.*

THE BEASTS OF THE PAST

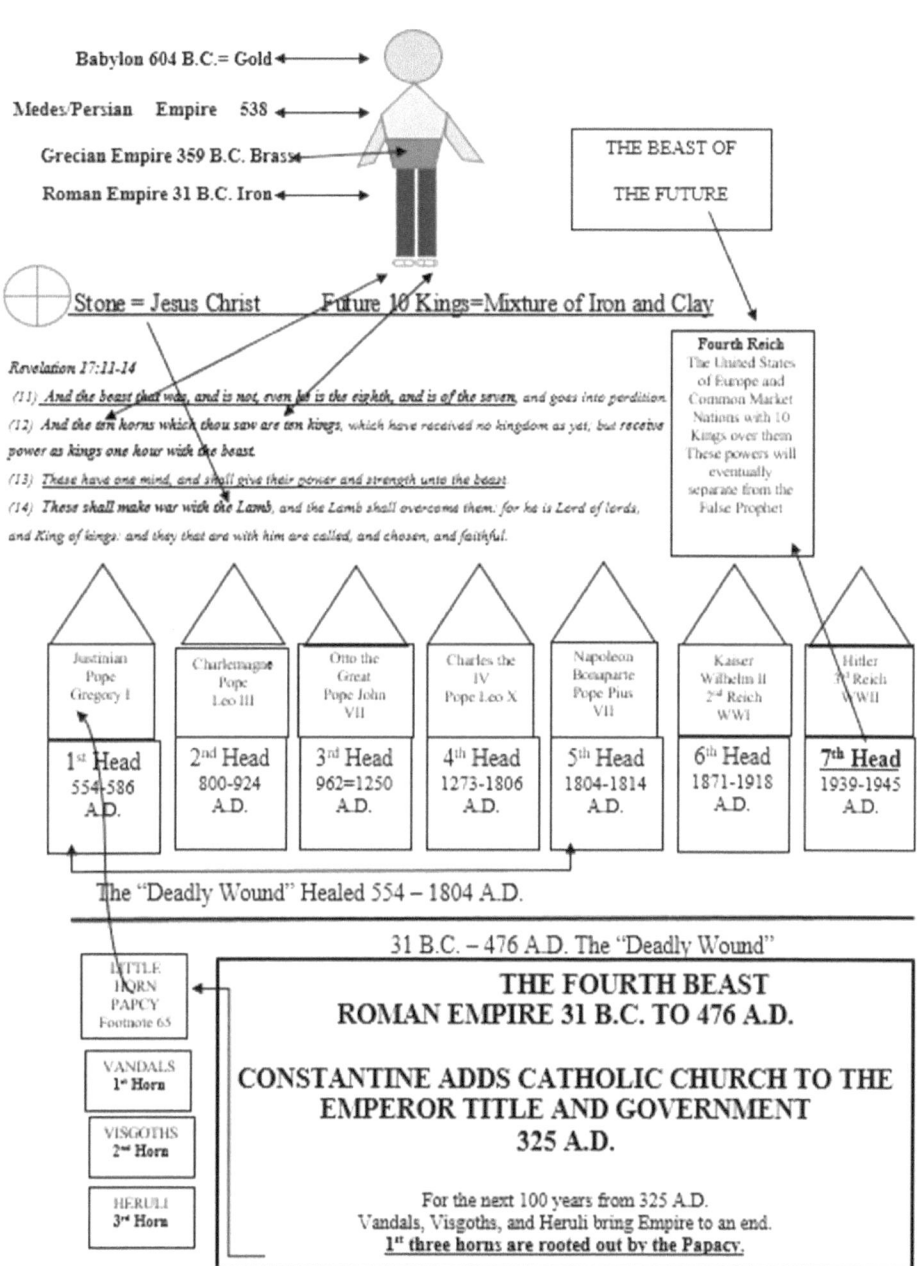

CHAPTER FOUR

FALSE PROPHET/BEAST POWER AND NEW WORLD ORDER

Since the Catholic Popes and its church was absorbed into the **Second Reich in 1871**, it has remained somewhat of a mysterious relationship with Germany. <u>Hitler was not catholic but used the religion to his advantage while waging worldwide war</u>. He saw himself as the *"protector of the church"* if it served his needs.

The post WWII Nazis dreamed of a united Europe with nations joining Germany in a U.S. of Europe, of course dominated by the Germans. They dreamed of a 'Common Market' a post war confederation within a common legal and currency system. Hitlerism was a burden due to his neo-paganism. They felt that could be overcome by a **Christian Germany** with <u>its roots firmly in the Reich concept as the protector of Christianity.</u>

Prince Lowenstein once said, <u>*"If only our voice could be joined with that of the* **Vatican***, which today forms the one point of stability in the general madness. I wish Catholics of all nations would unite. This Protestantism is a forerunner of atheism and has forced millions out of the Christian community."*</u>

Lowenstein and his constituents feel a Fourth German Reich will rise to fulfill the history of all its centuries, a German Reich in whose golden eagles are alive with the idea of social, political, and spiritual liberty.

Speculation

As the European Union evolves into a dictatorship, (*and I believe it will*) it will begin to reach back to its <u>Roman roots and Holy Roman</u>

mannerisms. It will seek out to use many of the symbols of history. Economic power will be part of its dominance. Euro Dollar vs American Dollar. They will revert to ancient symbolism of old European Traditions.

They could adopt the Double Eagle as symbolic Western and Eastern Europe cooperation. They would of course include Israel with 12 stones standing for the tribes of Israel. The cross would be an especially important symbol. These along with the "Spear of Destiny" the one that pierced Christ live today in the Treasure House, Vienna. They would be used to decorate the Leadership of the New World Order and fulfill the dream of world peace.

Humanity has always had a problem with the invisible, so these objects would be revered by all who see them in play. All the former Holy Roman Emperors wore or used these in some manner as representing the god of the heavens.

The Pope would begin to champion peace in the Middle East and create a bond worldwide. This last Pope, Francis, was only the 4th to visit Jerusalem in all these centuries. The Catholic church is becoming more and more interested in the affairs of the Middle East and Jerusalem. If they broker a peace in this center of so much conflict, think what a powerful witness that would be for a New World Order.

You can be sure when the New World Order or New Holy Roman Empire or the "*Eighth of the Seventh*" comes there will be pomp and ceremony beyond belief. There will be military parades and pageants of symbolism drawing on the history of Europe and its many Holy Empires.

Former Chancellor Helmut Kohl explicitly said: *"The future will belong to the Germans—when we build the house of Europe."*

In the 1950's Hans Seebohm a member pf the Adenauer government said: *"Germany is the heart of Europe, and the limbs must adapt themselves to the heart."*

Since 1989 with the downing of the post WWII Berlin wall, Berlin is now the official capital of Germany.

As I showed in a former chapter of this book, proclivities of a nation may be dormmate for a while, but they will rise from time to time. The day will come when GERMANY and the EUROPEAN UNION will become the world's supreme power on earth and promote the philosophy in a Fourth Reich. **The New World Order!** Economics and world trade will be a major factor! [70]Nations who do not have the "Mark" will not be able to trade goods.

Today, right under the Angelo/Saxon nation's noses, a United States of Europe is being forged, a revived Holy Roman Empire controlled by the "Father land" and "Mother" church of Europe. History will repeat itself yet again with a Catholic/German union that will try to **control the economics and people of the world**.

(This divided city of Berlin in Germany had impeded Europe from restoring her vast Empire. The destruction of that wall reunited Germany once again.)

What the Germans Say About Their Role in European Common Market

The German news magazine **_Der Spiegel_** mentioned the concept of the **Fourth Reich** in a 2015 editorial:

"People have even begun talking about the 'Fourth Reich,' a reference to the Third Reich of Adolf Hitler. That may sound absurd given that today's Germany is a successful democracy without a trace of <u>National Socialism</u> -- and that no one would actually associate Chancellor Merkel with Nazism. But further reflection on the word 'Reich,' or empire, may not be entirely out of place. The term refers to a dominion, with a central power exerting control over many different peoples. According to this definition, would it be wrong to speak of a German Reich in the economic realm?"

Historical Information / Concepts of a Fourth Reich

The **Fourth Reich** (German: *Viertes Reich*) is a hypothetical future German Reich that is the successor to Third Reich (1933–1945), following traditional order introduced in Arthur Moeller van den Bruck's 1923 book *Das Dritte Reich* that included the Holy Roman Empire of the German Nation as the First Reich, and the German Empire as the Second Reich.

---

[70] ***Deuteronomy 6:4***
(4) Hear, O Israel: The LORD our God is one LORD:

The term Third Reich was coined by Arthur Moeller van den Bruck as the title of his 1923 book *Das Dritte Reich*. It refers to Nazi Germany. It was used by the Nazis for propaganda purposes to legitimize their regime as a successor state to the retroactively-renamed First Reich (the Holy Roman Empire, 962–1806) and the Second Reich (Imperial Germany, 1871–1918). The terms "First Reich" and "Second Reich" were never used by historians.

The term **"Fourth Reich"** has been used in a variety of unusual ways. Neo-Nazis have used it to describe their envisioned revival of Nazi Germany, while others have used the term derogatorily, such as conspiracy theorists like Dr. Joseph P. Farrell, Peter Levenda, and Jim Marrs who have The United States of Europe is widely hypothesized, fictionalized or depicted as a superpower that is as powerful as, or more powerful than, the United States. Some people, such as T.R. Reid, **Andrew Redding and Mark Leonard, believe that the power of the hypothetical United States of Europe will rival that of the United States in the twenty-first century**. Leonard cites seven factors: Europe's large population, Europe's large economy, Europe's low inflation rates, Europe's central location in the world, the unpopularity and perceived failure of American foreign policy in recent years and certain European countries' highly developed social organization and quality of life (when measured in terms such as hours worked per week and income distribution). Some experts claim that Europe has developed a sphere of influence called the "*Euro sphere*" and used it to refer to what they perceive as a covert continuation of Nazi ideals, and by **critics who believe that Germany exercises a dominant role in the European Union.**

In terms of neo-Nazism, the **Fourth Reich** is envisioned as featuring Aryan supremacy, anti-Semitism, *Lebensraum*, aggressive militarism and totalitarianism. Upon the establishment of the **Fourth Reich**, German neo-Nazis propose that Germany should acquire nuclear weapons and use the threat of their use as a form of nuclear blackmail to re-expand to Germany's former boundaries as of 1937. (*Scary situation*)

Based on pamphlets published by David Myatt in the early 1990s, many neo-Nazis came to believe that the rise of the **Fourth Reich in Germany** would pave the way for the establishment of the *Western*

Imperium, a pan-Aryan world empire encompassing all land populated by predominantly European-descended peoples (i.e., Europe, Russia, Anglo-America, Australia, South America's Southern Cone, New Zealand, South Africa).

United Kingdom (*an Israelitish nation with roots back to Ephraim, Joseph's son*)

(As I was authoring this book, the UK voted to withdraw from the European Union)

British conservative and Eurosceptic journalist Simon Heffer wrote in the *Daily Mail* in 2011: *"Where Hitler failed by military means to conquer Europe, modern Germans are succeeding through trade and financial discipline. Welcome to the Fourth Reich".*

Political commentator Simon Heffer wrote in The Telegraph 2016: "*Cameron plainly won't admit that German domination of the EU means it has conquered without war, and signing up to the EU is signing up to the Fourth Reich. Ask the Greeks if you think I exaggerate* **Germany runs Europe without firing a shot**. *It forces far weaker partners to stay in a currency zone that is crippling them and uses its* **economic muscle** *to dictate immigration and other key policies.*

If you believe the Germans won't take a UK vote to stay in as a signal to continue and intensify their control over the EU, and to make us help pay for its baleful effects, then you aren't paying attention. **It's not war we should fear, but what the Germans do in times of peace.**"

In 2016 the journalist Johnny Sjöblom published a Swedish language article in YLE titled **"Merkel's Germany: Fourth Reich?"**. Sjöblom wrote: *"As a result of the economic crisis in the euro area, the German issue has again appeared on the agenda, some researchers argue.* **Germany has again become too big and powerful for Europe.** *During the current crisis, Germany has pursued its own will at the expense of others."*

This is a *"wait and see process"* that will slowly develop as time goes by. But make no mistake, it is possible for the dollar to lose world status and the Euro Mark replace it some time in our future. This will be an economic disaster for America. Trillions of dollars in debt to other countries could begin its decline as an economic power player in the world.

Personal Speculation: Could this be the first 3.5 years before the 3.5 years of Great Tribulation?

The bible predicts a time of peace for Jerusalem just before the Great Tribulation.

BABYLON WILL FALL

The coming New World Order is the same system that was created by Nimrod and others after the flood of Noah's time. It involves mysteries and control of people and nations. All roads lead back to the Original Babylon. In my first book, **Why You Were Born**, I outlined the treachery contrived by bad people. God eventually confused the languages at the Tower of Babel to scatter the peoples all over the world. Now, almost 4,000 years later, the language barrier is broken, and the world is still in chaos because of man's lust for power and control.

It is sad to see in history the many false things that the Babylonian Mystery Religion has put upon humanity. <u>The very mysteries of the Catholic Church have their roots in these Babylonian Traditions, ceremonies, and symbols.</u>

These mysterious religious practices remained among the heathens and pagans for centuries. Then soon after Christ came and showed us the true God, these mysteries were grafted into Christianity and perverted its true meaning. <u>Constantine mixed paganism with Christianity and called it *"Christianity."* Jesus warned us this would happen. His apostles warned us this would happen.</u>[71]

The Catholic Church Today

In 1989 the Catholic Pope has a 30-minute conversation with the Leader of Russia and the Berlin Wall comes down. This reunifies the German peoples once again!

---

[71] Rom 1:18

(18) For the wrath of God is revealed from heaven against all ungodliness and unrighteousness of men, who hold the truth in unrighteousness;

MAN'S RELIGION AND GOVERNMENT FOR THE NATIONS REVEALING THE RELIGIOUS SYSTEM OF BABYLON

This is a painful look at the absolute truth of the Mystery Religion, adopted by the Holy Roman Catholic Church, which has dominated the world since the days of Nimrod. When scriptures are searched and the more minutely studied, truth rises to the top and is undeniable for the Christian relying on the Holy Spirit to guide them into the truth.

The study of prophecy in Scripture makes sense as prophetic symbols lay the groundwork and become the corner stone of understanding the present-day religions and governments of men.

NOTE: This is not an attack on good religious people of all faiths; it is a historical fact of the origin of **Roman Religious Church leadership**. We have the freedom to worship however we please. There has never been any difficulty in the mind of any Christian with the Holy Spirit guidance to name the woman *"sitting on seven mountains,"* and has on her forehead the name. written, **"MYSTERY BABYLON THE GREAT."**

Revelation 17:3-6 So he carried me away in the spirit into the wilderness: and I saw a woman sit upon a scarlet-colored beast, full of names of blasphemy, **having seven heads and ten horns**. *(4) And the woman was arrayed in purple and scarlet color, and decked with gold and precious stones and pearls, having a golden cup in her hand full of abominations and filthiness of her fornication: (5) And upon her forehead was a name written,* **MYSTERY, BABYLON THE GREAT, THE MOTHER OF HARLOTS AND ABOMINATIONS OF THE EARTH**. *(6) And I saw the woman drunken with the blood of the saints, and with the blood of the martyrs of Jesus: and when I saw her, I wondered with great admiration.*

The scripture is very plain and direct. While the characteristic of Rome has not been well marked and defined, it is quite easy to see that the "Church" aspect of Rome has its seat. and headquarters on seven hills of Rome. In **324 A.D. Emperor Constantine** sets up the Eastern headquarters as a city with seven hills also, Constantinople. (*Do not confuse these seven hills with the seven mountains of prophetic language. The seven* mountains prophetically are. seven kingdoms that come out of Rome after its fall in 476 A.D.)

It is not wrong to say the Roman Catholic system of religion is based on many of the traditions practiced by the ancient Babylonian religion. We know without a doubt that Popery is merely baptized Paganism. (*Worship of a man*) History makes it clear that this church is the church of Babylon as God's word fitly describes her. Rome is the Babylon of the Apocalypse; the essential character of her system, the objects of her worship, festivals, doctrines, and disciplines mirror the ancient **Mystery Religion.** The Pope is the lineal line of Belshazzar.

Daniel 5:1-4 Belshazzar the king made a great feast to a thousand of his lords and drank wine before the thousand. (2) Belshazzar, while he tasted the wine, commanded to bring the golden and silver vessels which his father Nebuchadnezzar had taken out of the temple which was in Jerusalem; that the king, and his princes, his wives, and his concubines, might drink there. (3) Then they brought the golden vessels that were taken out of the temple of the house of God which was at Jerusalem; and the king, and his princes, his wives, and his concubines, drank in them. (4) They drank wine, and praised the gods of gold, and of silver, of brass, of iron, of wood, and of stone.

Babylon is the woman with the **golden cup in her hand**. The shape of the cup is the same as the cup held in the hand of the **Assyrian kings.** (Remember, **Ancient Assyrians are ancestors of the Germans**) The **Chaldean queen** is a fit and remarkable prototype of the *"woman"* in the Apocalypse holding a golden cup in her hand deceiving the nations.

This is the symbolic woman John sees as the *"mother of harlots"* *"drunken with the blood of the saints."* One only needs to read Fox's book of Martyrs to make the connection about the blood of saints. (Prophetic metaphor for church is woman or mother.) She rides the BEAST.

In **1825, the Roman Church takes this very symbol**, woman with the cup, as her own chosen emblem. **Pope Leo XII** strikes a medal, bearing on one side his own image and the Church of Rome on the other. A woman holding in her left-hand a cross, and in her right-hand a cup. It is surrounded with the inscription *"Sedet super universum."* Translated, "**the whole world is her seat.**"

From its start, this religion is designed to bind all humanity in blind and absolute submission to a hierarchy entirely dependent on the sovereigns of the church, or in modern times, the Pope. People are bound neck and heel to the priests. In ancient times Priests are the only depositaries of religious knowledge. They have the traditions by which the writs and symbols of public religion can be interpreted. By the time, Jesus is here and gone, saints are sealing their testimony for the truth with their own blood. At the very beginning of the age of the apostles the "Mystery of Iniquity" as Paul calls it, is hard at work.

2Thessalonians 2:7 For the mystery of iniquity doth already work: only he who now let's will let, until he be taken out of the way.

It's not that hard to see the rebellion toward the true religion Jesus teaches. James the half-brother of Jesus says, *"confess your faults to one another,"* the Catholic church says, *"confess them to the priests."*

James 5:16 Confess your faults one to another, and pray one for another, that ye may be healed. The effectual fervent prayer of a righteous man avails much. Jesus says, *"call no man on earth Father,"* the Catholic church says, *"call your priests father."*

Matthew 23:9 And call no man your father upon the earth: for one is your Father, which is in heaven.

Jesus says, *"the seventh day is the day of rest,"* the Catholic church says, *"Sunday is the Lord's Day and a day of worship."*

HOW THE TRINITY CONCEPT ORIGINATED

It should be becoming clear that Babylon is the source of all false religion. Jeremiah says it a plain as any prophet.

Jeremiah 51:7 Babylon hath been a golden cup in the LORD'S hand, which made all the earth drunken: the nations have drunken of her wine; therefore, **the nations are mad**.

I should note that the word <u>mad</u> in this scripture does not mean angry. It means crazy! It is the English word for the Hebrew word: *hâlal haw-lal.'*

A primitive root; to make a show; to boast; and thus, to be (clamorously) foolish; to rave; causatively to celebrate; also, to stultify: - (make) boast (self), celebrate, commend, (deal, make), fool (-ish, -ly), glory, give [light], be (make, feign self) mad (against),

No other church service has as much boasting and ritual show of will worship as a Catholic Mass. It is centered around the priest and objects of worship. Most historians will tell you that the religious system of Egypt is derived from Asia, and the primitive empire in Babel. Nimrod and Semiramis. What we end up with is a mixture of Egyptian, Assyrian, Greek and Roman religious systems based on idolatry and mysterious rituals.

This is not always the case in the earlier times. The unity of one God is long believed by many of the pagan religions. They distinctly acknowledge that there is one infinite and almighty Creator, supreme overall. The existence of a sole and omnipotent Deity, who creates all things, is a universal belief, in the early ages of humanity. **The Icelandic mythology calls God** *"the Author of everything that exists, the eternal, the living, and awful Being: the searcher into concealed things, the Being that never changes."* The ancients attributed the deity of God *"an infinite power, a boundless knowledge, and incorruptible justice."*

Though modern Hinduism recognizes many gods, the Indian sacred books show that originally it was far otherwise. Their original god, Brahm, the supreme god of the Hindoos is recognized as "one whose glory is so great, there is no image; He illumines all, delights all the very name they chose, Brahm, means one infinite and eternal God. They even say that all beings are created by His mouth or word. (As does the bible narrative)

The bible asserts the Unity of the Godhead in emphatic language. [72]*"Hear, O Israel, Jehovah our God is one Jehovah."*

The Babylonians begin to characterize God as One in three persons. They choose the Triangle as their symbol for this concept. The same symbol is used by the Roman Catholic church today. It is an inspired belief to degrade the One Omnipotent God Almighty. The Papacy in some of its churches such as the Monastery called Trinitarians of Madrid, display an image of a Triune God, with three heads on one body. *Genesis 1:27 So*

---

[72] ***Daniel 12:8-10***

(8) And I heard, but I understood not: then said I, O my Lord, what shall be the end of these things?
(9) And he said, go thy way, Daniel: for the words are closed and sealed till the time of the end.
(10) Many shall be purified, and made white, and tried; but the wicked shall do wickedly: and none of the wicked shall understand; but the wise shall understand.

God created man in his own image, in the image of God created he him; male and female created he them. (We do not have one body with three heads)

This concept is spread over the nations for centuries. In India, their supreme deity is represented with one body, three heads, called, **Eko Deva Trimurtti**, translated, "One God, three forms." In Japan, they worship the divinity Buddha, with three heads under the name, **San Pao Fuh.** All these have existed from the times of ancient Babylon.

Though this is how Pagan Idolatry stands for the Triune God, the Catholic Church changes it to become three persons known as the Eternal Father, the Spirit of God incarnate in a human mother, and a Divine Son, the fruit of that incarnation. The corruption is. like a cancer infecting many nations throughout history.

The Protestants are no more the wiser than Catholics. They teach their version of Trinity.

Doctrine as, Father, Son, Holy Spirit as three persons.

[73]This information is first brought into light in **1853** and has long been swept. under the carpet of deceit and lethargic preachers for years. I bring it up to make the point. of **why there will be Armageddon** and why **the bible teaches the destruction of this religious system when Christ returns.** The following scriptures denote how God views this equal. triangular, divinity deity concept, **called the Trinity Doctrine.**

Psalms 113:5 Who is like unto the LORD our God, who dwells on high,

Isaiah 40:25 To whom then will ye liken me, or shall I be equal? says the Holy One.

Isaiah 46:5 To whom will ye liken me, and make me equal, and compare me, that we may be like?

John 6:38

---

[73] **Daniel 12:8-10** And I heard, but I understood not: then said I, O my Lord, what shall be the end of these things? (9) And he said, Go thy way, Daniel: *for the words are closed up and sealed till the time of the end.* (10) Many shall be purified, and made white, and tried; but the wicked shall do wickedly: and none of the wicked shall understand; but the wise shall understand.

(38) For I came down from heaven, not to do mine own will, but the will of him that sent me.

It would take another whole book to cover all the corrupt doctrines and deceit that has been. taught to unsuspecting believers who do not study the bible and its information for themselves.

THE HOLY SEE

Every **See** is considered holy. In Greek, the adjective *"holy"* or *"sacred"* (ιερά transliterated as *hiera*) is constantly applied to all such Sees as a matter of course. In the West, the adjective is not commonly added, but it does form part of an official title of the Diocese of Rome ("**the Holy See**") The Vicar of Christ, what blasphemy. Self-worship.

Remember the **Fourth Beast is a World Dominating force** down through time. It is a military force that subdues nations, and it is influences by the Religious Prophet or *"See."* This beast is created in **31 B.C.** and is enormously powerful during the time of Christ. It handles changing the things Christ teaches in the Gospel of Salvation for the world. According to the scriptures this terrible beast is wounded to death, resurrected by five different heads, during the times of the Holy Roman Church and Papacy having influence over it. Now we are at a point in history when the Holy Roman Church and Papacy take a non-secular religious posture independent from the world powers, incognito. (In other words, they are not now pushing the beast domination of the world; they are making converts all over the world of the people of any nation.) Not unlike the ancient Babylonians, they have become subtle in their influencing the peoples of the nations.

The word *"See"* comes from the Latin word *"sedes"*, meaning *"seat"*, which refers to the Episcopal throne (cathedra). The term *"Apostolic See"* can refer to any See founded by one of the Apostles, but, when used with the definite article, it is used in the Catholic Church to refer specifically to the See of the Bishop of Rome, whom that Church promotes Sees as successor of Saint Peter, the Prince of the Apostles. (In my first book; Why You Were Born, I proved that Peter is never in Rome nor Christ appoint him to be the head of any Roman Church.) The Pope assumes the "chair of authority" of Christ on earth.

Although the **Holy See** is closely associated with the Vatican City, the independent territory over which the **Holy See is sovereign**, the two entities are separate and distinct. After the Italians takeover of the Papal States in 1870, the **Holy See has no territorial sovereignty**. In spite of some uncertainty among jurists as to whether it could continue to act as an independent personality in international matters, the Holy See continues in fact to exercise the right to send and receive diplomatic representatives, maintaining relations with states that include the major powers of Russia, Prussia and Austria-Hungary. Where, in accordance with the decision of the **1815 Congress of Vienna**,

VATICAN Sovereign Created

The **State of the Vatican City** is created by the **Lateran Treaty in 1929** to *"ensure the absolute and visible independence of the Holy See"* and *"to guarantee to it an indisputable sovereignty in international affairs."* Untouchable power! Archbishop Jean-Louis Tauran, the Holy See's former Secretary for Relations with States, said that the Vatican City is a *"minuscule support-state that guarantees the spiritual freedom of the Pope with the minimum territory"*.

The Holy See, not Vatican City, keeps diplomatic relations with states. Foreign embassies are accredited to the Holy See, not to the Vatican City, and it is the Holy See that establishes treaties and concordats with other sovereign entities. When necessary, the Holy See will enter a treaty on behalf of the Vatican City.

Under the terms of the Lateran Treaty, the Holy See has extraterritorial authority over various sites in Rome and two Italian sites outside of Rome, including the Pontifical Palace at Castel Gandolfo. The same authority is extended under international law over the Apostolic Nunciature of the Holy See in a foreign country.

Though, like various European powers, earlier Popes recruit Swiss mercenaries as part of an army, the Pontifical Swiss Guard is founded by Pope Julius II on 22 January 1506 as the personal bodyguard of the Pope and continues to fulfil that function. It is listed in the Annuaries under "**Holy See**", not under "**State of Vatican City**" All recruits must be Catholic, unmarried males with Swiss citizenship who have completed their basic training with the Swiss Armed Forces with certificates of good conduct, be between the ages of 19 and 30, and be at least 175 cm (5 ft. 9 in) in height. Members are armed with small arms and the traditional halberd (also called the Swiss voulge) and trained in bodyguarding tactics.

The Pope governs the Catholic Church through the **Roman Curia**. The Roman Curia consists of a complex of offices that administer church affairs at the highest level, including the Secretariat of State, nine Congregations, three Tribunals, eleven Pontifical Councils, and seven Pontifical Commissions. The Secretariat of State, under the Cardinal Secretary of State, directs and coordinates the Curia the Secretariat of State is the only body of the Curia that is situated within Vatican City. The others are in buildings in parts of Rome that have extraterritorial rights like those of embassies.

Among the most active of the major Curial institutions are the Congregation for the Doctrine of the Faith, which oversees the Catholic Church's doctrine; the Congregation for Bishops, which coordinates the appointment of bishops worldwide; the Congregation for the Evangelization of Peoples, which oversees all missionary activities; and the Pontifical Council for Justice and Peace, which deals with international peace and social issues.

The Holy See does not dissolve upon a Pope's death or resignation. It instead operates under a separate set of laws *sede vacante*. During this interregnum, the heads of the dicasteries of the Roman Curia (such as the prefects of congregations) cease immediately to hold office, the only exceptions being the Major Penitentiary, who continues his important role regarding absolutions and dispensations, and the Camerlengo of the Holy Roman Church, The Holy See has been recognized, both in state practice and in the writing of modern legal scholars, as a subject of public international law, with rights and duties analogous to those of States.

Although the **Holy See**, as distinct from the **Vatican City State**, does not fulfill the long-established criteria in international law of statehood—having a permanent population, a defined territory, a stable government and the capacity to enter into relations with other states, its possession of full legal personality in international law is shown by the fact that it maintains diplomatic relations with 180 states, that it is a *member-state* in various intergovernmental international organizations, and that it is: "respected by the international community of sovereign States and treated as a subject of international law having the capacity to engage in diplomatic relations and to enter into binding agreements with one, several, or many states under international law that are largely geared to establish and preserving peace in the world.

Since medieval times the episcopal see of Rome has been recognized as a sovereign entity. The Holy See (not the State of Vatican City) maintains formal diplomatic relations with and for the most recent establishment of diplomatic relations with 183 sovereign states, and with the European Union. The Holy See is a member of various International organizations and groups including the International Atomic Energy Agency.

Can you see how the power of the church with the False Prophet is going to eventually be a problem for the **Beast Power** as their cooperation becomes a rival for power? The bible predicts that the Beast will destroy the church's authority and sit on the throne of the Temple itself. ***Revelation 17:16***

*(16) And the ten horns which thou saw upon the beast, these **shall hate the whore, and shall make her desolate and naked, and shall eat her flesh, and burn her with fire**.*

CHRIST WILL DESTROY THIS SYSTEM WHEN HE COMES

Revelation 18:2-24

*(2) And he cried mightily with a strong voice, saying, **Babylon the great is fallen**, is fallen, and is become the habitation of devils, and the hold of every foul spirit, and a cage of every unclean and hateful bird.*

(3) For all nations have drunk of the wine of the wrath of her fornication, and the kings of the earth have committed fornication with her, and the merchants of the earth are waxed rich through the abundance of her delicacies.

*(4) And I heard another voice from heaven, saying, **Come out of her, my people, that ye be not partakers of her sins, and that ye receive not of her plagues**.*

(5) For her sins have reached unto heaven, and God hath remembered her iniquities.

(6) Reward her even as she rewarded you, and double unto her double according to her works: in the cup which she hath filled fill to her double.

(7) *How much she hath glorified herself, and lived deliciously, so much torment and sorrow give her: for she saith in her heart, I sit a queen, and am no widow, and shall see no sorrow.*

(8) *Therefore shall her plagues come in one day, death, and mourning, and famine;* **and she shall be utterly burned with fire: for strong is the Lord God who judges her.**

(9) **And the kings of the earth, who have committed fornication and lived deliciously with her,** *shall bewail her, and lament for her, when they shall see the smoke of her burning,*

(10) *Standing afar off for the fear of her torment, saying, Alas, alas, that great city Babylon, that mighty city! for in one hour is thy judgment come.*

(11) *And the merchants of the earth shall weep and mourn over her; for no man buys their merchandise any more:*

(12) *The merchandise of gold, and silver, and precious stones, and of pearls, and fine linen, and purple, and silk, and scarlet, and all thine wood, and all manner vessels of ivory, and all manner vessels of most precious wood, and of brass, and iron, and marble,*

(13) *And cinnamon, and odors, and ointments, and frankincense, and wine, and oil, and fine flour, and wheat, and beasts, and sheep, and horses, and chariots, and slaves, and souls of men.*

(14) *And the fruits that thy soul lusted after are departed from thee, and all things which were dainty and goodly are departed from thee, and thou shalt find them no more at all.*

(15) *The merchants of these things, which were made rich by her, shall stand afar off for the fear of her torment, weeping and wailing,*

(16) *And saying, Alas, alas, that great city, that was clothed in fine linen, and purple, and scarlet, and decked with gold, and precious stones, and pearls!*

(17) *For in one hour so great riches is come to nothing. And every shipmaster, and all the company in ships, and sailors, and as many as trade by sea, stood afar off,*

(18) *And cried when they saw the smoke of her burning, saying, What city is like unto this great city!*

(19) *And they cast dust on their heads, and cried, weeping and wailing, saying, Alas, alas, that great city, wherein were made rich all that had ships in the sea by reason of her costliness! for in one hour is she made desolate.*

*(20) **Rejoice over her, thou heaven, and ye holy apostles and prophets; for God hath avenged you on her.***

*(21) And a mighty angel took up a stone like a great millstone, and cast it into the sea, saying, **Thus with violence shall that great city Babylon be thrown down, and shall be found no more at all.***

(22) And the voice of harpers, and musicians, and of pipers, and trumpeters, shall be heard no more at all in thee; and no craftsman, of whatsoever craft he be, shall be found any more in thee; and the sound of a millstone shall be heard no more at all in thee;

*(23) And the light of a candle shall shine no more at all in thee; and the voice of the bridegroom and of the bride shall be heard no more at all in thee: for thy merchants were the great men of the earth; **for by thy sorceries were all nations deceived**.*

*(24) **And in her was found the blood of prophets, and of saints, and of all that were slain upon the earth.***

This is the end of the Mystery Religion that has deceived the people and nations all down through the centuries. It is part of the Armageddon scenario for the False church.

This information is necessary to help understand why there must be a Battle of Armageddon to put down these wicked leaders and systems of government and religion they foster.

The next chapter is detailing the prophesies of the book of Revelation. It can get confusing at times. When it does, I just put it aside and ask God for peace of mind and go back to it later. This is powerful truth not found in religious books. It is a spiritual thing, and it is taxing on the mind. Please do not be discouraged, for there is a great outcome at the end of these events.

CHAPTER FIVE

Exploring The "Latter Days" Prophesies

The book of **Revelation** is extraordinarily complex and requires a dedicated amount of research and study to interpret the language and scattered events. The overall world conditions and spiritual aspects are centered around the **Seven Seals**. [74]This is the information sealed up from Daniel and revealed to the apostle John 600 years later by an angel from Jesus; sometime around 100 A. D.

This will be a detailed study of Revelation and the many aspects of events worldwide and heavenly. Some have been going on since Christ revealed them and some are yet to come. It is important to remember that the Apostle John saw these visions in dreams and wrote them down as he could remember. Most of it was difficult for him to describe in the language of his day. Therefore, much of the language is metaphoric. This is the information sealed up from Daniel.

It is important to note that these prophetic seals are only revealed by Jesus Christ. This is detailed information that enhances what Daniel wrote over 500 years before Jesus tells his disciples in on the Mount of Olives shortly before His crucifixion, and what John wrote what he sees in vision in the book of Revelation of Jesus Christ.

---

[74] ***Revelation 20:5*** *But the rest of the dead lived not again until the thousand years were finished. This is the first resurrection.*

The Revelation of Jesus Christ to His Believers

This will be a detailed, verse by verse, interpretation of the visions of the Apostle John from an angel sent by Jesus Christ. It is important to understand that there are companion scriptures that must be considered to understand and see the overall events described in the book of Revelation. In the introduction of the book of Revelation John sees some heavenly visions revealing the ongoing circumstances since Jesus was born into the family of God as the "*first begotten*" and then "*first-born*" Son of God. In other words, God starts His family of Spirit Beings with His begotten Son. Jesus Christ is born of the virgin Mary and eventually was begotten by the Holy Spirit at the Jordon River. God announced him as His begotten Son. Eventually Jesus fulfills His mission on earth and is put to death then raised up as the First-Born Son of God and placed at the right side of God's throne in heaven.

[75]The book of Daniel has snippets of the information but not the details we find in the opening of the Seven Seals of Revelation. Unfortunately, many people "*blow off*" the book of Revelation as a nightmare from John the Apostle meant to scare the "*hell*" out of people. Not in the least! It is the *"Final Prophecy"* from Jesus Christ himself, sent through a messenger angel to John the Apostle for our information. When fully studied and understood it holds "*Good News*" for the believers in Jesus Christ.

The timeline for the information in Revelation will come into focus as we progress through the events of the Seven seals that are opened to us. Let us begin with the introduction to the book of Revelation. These Seven Seals will take us up to the return of Jesus Christ and Armageddon.

---

[75] Act 2:20 *The sun shall be turned into darkness, and the moon into blood, before that great and notable day of the Lord come:*

   1Co 5:5 *To deliver such an one unto Satan for the destruction of the flesh, that the spirit may be saved in the day of the Lord Jesus.*

   2Co 1:14 *As also ye have acknowledged us in part, that we are your rejoicing, even as ye also are ours in the day of the Lord Jesus.*

   1Th 5:2 *For yourselves know perfectly that the day of the Lord so cometh as a thief in the night.*

   2Pe 3:10 *But the day of the Lord will come as a thief in the night; in the which the heavens shall pass away with a great noise, and the elements shall melt with fervent heat, the earth also and the works that are therein shall be burned up.*

Revelation 1:1-3

(1) **The Revelation of Jesus Christ**, *which God gave unto him, to shew unto his servants things which must shortly come to pass; and* **He sent and signified it by his angel unto his servant John**: (It is the Revelation from Jesus Christ, not John the Apostle.)

(2) Who bare record of the word of God, and of **the testimony of Jesus Christ**, *and of all things that he saw.* (John the Apostle)

(3) Blessed is he that reads, and they that hear the words of this prophecy, and keep those things which are written therein: **for the time is at hand**. (This is a reference to us today, who believe in Jesus and the Holy Word of God, the bible. This happens all down thru history as people pick up the Word of God and believe. There was a great fight with the Holy Roman Church to even have a bible in the hands of the average person; another whole story.)

This first Revelation copy was sent to the existing Seven churches that were well set up in John's Day.

Revelation 1:4-7

(4) **John to the seven churches which are in Asia**: *Grace be unto you, and peace, from him which is, and which was, and which is to come; and from the seven Spirits which are before his throne;*

(5) And from Jesus Christ, who is the faithful witness, and the first begotten of the dead, and the prince of the kings of the earth. Unto him that loved us, and washed us from our sins in his own blood,

(6) And hath made us kings and priests unto God and his Father; to him be glory and dominion for ever and ever. Amen.

(7) Behold, he cometh with clouds; and every eye shall see him, and they also which pierced him: and all kindreds of the earth shall wail because of him. Even so, Amen.

[76](The statement "and they also which pierced Him;" is referring to a time after the millennium. More about this when we get through the timeline.)

---

[76] Letters to the Seven Churches of Asia

[77]The next verses are also a vision that John could see into the throne room of God. Now the next verses are not talking about a vision on Sunday for John. He was having a visionary dream at the time of the **Day of the Lord**, yet ahead in our future.

Revelation 1:9-20

(9) I John, who also am your brother, and companion in tribulation, and in the kingdom and patience of Jesus Christ, was in the isle that is called Patmos, for the word of God, and for the testimony of Jesus Christ.

(10) ***I was in the Spirit on the Lord's day****, and heard behind me a great voice, as of a trumpet,*

(11) Saying, I am Alpha and Omega, the first and the last: and, What thou see, write in a book,(This is the book of Revelation) *and send it unto the seven churches which are in Asia; unto Ephesus, and unto Smyrna, and unto Pergamos, and unto Thyatira, and unto Sardis, and unto Philadelphia, and unto Laodicea.*

(12) And I turned to see the voice that spoke with me. And being turned, ***I saw seven golden candlesticks;***

(13) And in the midst of ***the seven candlesticks*** *one like unto the Son of man, clothed with a garment down to the foot, and girt about the paps with a golden girdle.*

(14) His head and his hairs were white like wool, as white as snow; and his eyes were as a flame of fire;

(15) And his feet like unto fine brass, as if they burned in a furnace; and his voice as the sound of many waters.

(16) And he had in his right hand ***seven stars****: and out of his mouth went a sharp two edged sword: and his countenance was as the sun shineth in his strength.*

(17) And when I saw him, I fell at his feet as dead. And he laid his right hand upon me, saying unto me, Fear not; ***I am the first and the last****:*

(18) I am he that lives, ***and was dead****; and, behold, I am alive for evermore, Amen; and have the keys of hell and of death.*

---

[77]   **Matthew 24:4-5** *And Jesus answered and said unto them,* **Take heed that no man deceive you.** *(5)* **For many shall come in my name, saying, I am Christ;** *(they are not saying they are Christ but preaching their version of who Christ is and what He is about) and shall deceive many.*

(19) Write the things which thou hast seen, and the things which are, and the things which shall be hereafter;

*(20) **The mystery** of the **seven stars** which thou saw in my right hand, and the **seven golden candlesticks. The seven stars are the angels of the seven churches: and the seven candlesticks which thou saw are the seven churches.*** (The bible often interprets itself if we read far enough)

When studied in detail, these seven churches are a footprint of attitudes and problems all churches down through time have met. These Seven churches in Asia are being cited as examples of what churches should and should not be. There is an angel over these churches; this could be true today of churches, the bible isn't specific on that.

[78]The next two chapters in Revelation, 2 and 3 address the good and bad points of churches. It is an interesting read when you have time.

Revelation chapter 4 is a scene depicting the throne room of God. Revelation chapter 5 is telling us that only Jesus is worthy to open the seals of information for the end time. This too is because it is close to His second return to earth. It is a glorious scene tied into the heavenly operations that go on unnoticed by humanity.

---

[78] *Hebrews 11:33-40*

(33) Who through faith subdued kingdoms, wrought righteousness, obtained promises, stopped the mouths of lions,

(34) Quenched the violence of fire, escaped the edge of the sword, out of weakness were made strong, waxed valiant in fight, turned to fight the armies of the aliens.

(35) Women received their dead raised to life again: and others were tortured, not accepting deliverance; that they might obtain a better resurrection:

(36) And others had trial of cruel mocking's and scourging's, yea, moreover of bonds and imprisonment:

(37) They were stoned, they were sawn asunder, were tempted, were slain with the sword: they wandered about in sheepskins and goatskins; being destitute, afflicted, tormented;

(38) (Of whom the world was not worthy:) they wandered in deserts, and in mountains, and in dens and caves of the earth.

(39) And these all, having obtained a good report through faith, received not the promise:

(40) God having provided some better thing for us, that they without us should not be made perfect.

Now let us turn to the first four of the seven seals. It is important to remember the events of the first four seals are present on the earth from the time of Christ until His second return. These seals stand for conditions on earth from the beginning of time. False religion, war, famine, and death are represented by the color of the four horses in the text. <u>These are the conditions that exist today and until Christ returns.</u>

THE FOUR HORSEMEN

An Ongoing Prophesy
First Four Seals

First let's consider the conditions on the earth as foretold by the four horsemen of the Apocalypse. False religion, wars, famine, disease, pestilence, and death have plagued humanity for centuries. These four seals are earthly conditions before and after the time of Christ.

The Four Horsemen are symbolic metaphors that suggest the conditions in the world that create the path to a final conflict between the forces of good and evil. This symbolism is used many times in prophetic writings. The metaphors used relate to the objects and things of the time of the prophecy is written. They are descriptive of the intent or things involved with the prophetic writing. These Four Horsemen of Revelation are the first four of Seven Seals opened in the revelation of future events in the Apostle John's vision from Jesus Christ. **<u>These symbolic Seals are spiritual information revealing the behavior and problems humanity brings upon itself, worldwide, until the "Last Days."</u>**

The White Horse:
- ➢ White horse, a symbol of purity and righteousness.
- ➢ Someone sitting on the white horse with a bow in his hands.
- ➢ He is given a crown.
- ➢ He goes out conquering and to conquer.

> *Revelation 6:1-2 And I saw when the Lamb opened one of the seals, and I heard, as it were the noise of thunder, one of the four beasts saying, See. (2) And I saw and behold a white horse: and he that sat on him had a bow; and a crown was given unto him: and he went forth conquering, and to conquer.*

This would seem to be a vision of Jesus Christ coming to conquer the Gentile Kingdoms of humanity as prophesied in the book of Daniel.

However, when we compare this vision with the things Jesus says to His disciples and look at what Jesus reveals to John in the 19th chapter of Revelation; we will see the truth in what this First Seal stands for.

FALSE RELIGIONS

[79]This first seal reveals there is a time of false religions influencing the peoples of the world. This is done under the flag of "Christianity." It is started by Constantine the Great, whom the world calls the "father of Christianity." Constantine was the first Roman emperor to convert to Christianity. Although he lived most of his life as a pagan, he claims the Christian faith on his deathbed, being baptized by Eusebius of Nicomedia. He plays an influential role in the proclamation of the Edict of Milan in 313, which declared religious tolerance for Christianity in the Roman empire. He calls the **First Council of Nicaea in 325** A.D. that produces the statement of Christian belief known as the **Nicene Creed**. The Church of the Holy Sepulcher is built on his orders at the purported site of Jesus' tomb in Jerusalem and becomes the holiest place in Christendom.

---

[79] *Jude 1:14-16*

(14) And Enoch also, the seventh from Adam, prophesied of these, saying, **Behold, the Lord cometh with ten thousands of his saints,**

(15) **To execute judgment upon all, and to convince all that are ungodly among them of all their ungodly deeds which they have ungodly committed, and of all their hard speeches which ungodly sinners have spoken against him.**

(16) These are murmurers, complainers, walking after their own lusts; and **their mouth speaks great swelling words,** *having men's persons in admiration because of advantage.*

The Papal claim to temporal power in the High Middle Ages is based on the supposed Donation of Constantine *(now regarded as a forgery)*. He is venerated as a saint by the Eastern Orthodox and Catholic Church. He has historically been referred to as the **"First Christian Emperor,"** and he did heavily promote the Christian Church. Some modern scholars, however, debate his beliefs and even his comprehension of the Christian faith itself. They do not check out how this great emperor operates and what his true intentions are with the acceptance of Christianity as his religion. The truth is, <u>Constantine is a pagan who is using his power to merge the truth of Christianity with paganism</u>. Paganisms and rituals that date all the way back to ancient Babylon, Nimrod and Semiramis; the founders of the Great Babylonian Mystery Religion.

> *Revelation 19:11-16 And **I saw heaven opened and behold a white horse**; and he that sat upon him was called **Faithful and True**, and in righteousness he doth judge and make war. (12) His eyes were as a flame of fire, and on his head, were many crowns; and he had a name written, that no man knew, but he himself. (13) And he was clothed with a vesture dipped in blood: and his name is called The Word of God. (14) And the armies which were in heaven followed him upon white horses, clothed in fine linen, white and clean. (15) And out of his mouth goes a sharp sword, that with it he should smite the nations: and he shall rule them with a rod of iron: and he treads the winepress of the fierceness and wrath of Almighty God. (16) And he hath on his vesture and on his thigh a name written, King of kings and Lord of lords.*

> *Jude 1:14-15 And Enoch also, the seventh from Adam, prophesied of these, saying, Behold, **the Lord cometh with ten-thousands of his saints**, (15) To execute judgment upon all, and to convince all that are ungodly among them of all their ungodly deeds which they have ungodly committed, and of all their hard speeches which ungodly sinners have spoken against him.*

There is no question this is Jesus Christ in Revelation 19.

- He is coming on a White Horse.
- He is named Faithful and True; He is also a judge.
- On His head are many crowns.
- He is clothed in a vesture dipped in blood.
- His name is The Word of God.
- He has a sword to smite the nations.
- He is followed by an army of saints on white horses, clothed in fine linen, white and clean.

What about the scene in Revelation 6? The white horse, a crown, and going out to conquer, what does this stand for?

To understand the First Seal opened by Jesus, we must look at the first things Jesus warns His disciples, in a private teaching, what to expect after He is crucified and ascended to heaven! As the information presents itself, you will begin to see **a parallel between what Jesus says in Matthew 24 and the Four Horsemen.**

Matthew 24:3-5 And as he sat upon the mount of Olives, the disciples came unto him privately, saying, tell us, when shall these things be? and what shall be the sign of thy coming, and of the end of the world? (4) And Jesus answered and said unto them, take heed that no man deceives you. (5) For many shall come in my name, saying, I am Christ; and shall deceive many.

Mark 13:3-6 And as he sat upon the mount of Olives over against the temple, Peter, James, John, and Andrew asked him privately, (4) Tell us, when shall these things be? and what shall be the sign when all these things shall be fulfilled? (5) And Jesus answering them began to say, take heed lest any man deceive you: (6) For many shall come in my name, saying, I am Christ; and shall deceive many.

Luke 21:7-8 And they asked him, saying, Master, but when shall these things be? and what sign will there be when these things shall come to pass? (8) And he said, take heed that ye be not deceived: for **many shall come in my name, saying, I am Christ**; *and the time draws near:* **go ye not therefore after them.**

When the disciples ask Christ when the things would come to pass and what would be the sign of His coming, Jesus does not answer their question! He at once warns them of something especially important; don't let yourselves be deceived about Me and My coming back! Some teach that Christ was saying many would come claiming to be Him! Well, yes and no! His intent is for them to understand **there will be many who would come professing** *"their version"* **of Jesus**; not necessarily claiming they were Jesus. As the world knows, the Pope claims Christ's title! He is proclaimed the vicar of Christ!

As the famous news commentator Paul Harvey used to say, *"and now for the rest of the story,"* let's consider what is the main warning of the Apostle Paul's writings to the true believers.

2 Corinthians 11:13-15 *For such are false apostles, deceitful workers, transforming themselves into the apostles of Christ. (14) And no marvel; for Satan, himself is transformed into an angel of light. (15) Therefore, it is no great thing if his ministers also be transformed as the ministers of righteousness; whose end shall be per their works.*

He is saying there will be impostors in their time and on down through time who will claim they are speaking on behalf of Jesus or are His personal representative on earth!

> ***2Thessalonians 2:2-3*** *That ye be not soon shaken in mind, or be troubled, neither by spirit, nor by word, nor by letter as from us, as that the day of Christ is at hand. (3) Let no man deceive you by any means: for that day shall not come, except there comes a falling away first, and that man of sin be revealed, the son of perdition.*

He is saying some men will go so far in the time of the true living apostles that they will use letters or decrees sent to the believers and churches as though it is from the apostles Jesus sent forth. **In our day, this is calling propaganda!** Promoting information for some cause, in this case false information about the ***"Faith once delivered by Christ and His Apostles!"***

THE RED HORSE
The Second Seal Opened
- The Red Horse is symbolic of War and bloodshed.

- ➢ The rider is given power to take peace from the earth.
- ➢ He causes the nations to kill one another.
- ➢ He is a military force of power.
- ➢ He can be any of the War Lords of history, Nimrod, Sargon II, Hito, Hitler, Napoleon, etc.

Revelation 6:3-4 *And when he had opened the second seal, I heard the second beast say, Come and see. (4) And there went out another horse that was red: and power was given to him that sat thereon to take peace from the earth, and that they should kill one another: and there was given unto him a great sword.*

War has been the blight on nations of the world since the times of the flood. Its foundational motives are for religious and territorial domination. There have been more wars fought in the name of religion than for any reason. It has resulted in at least Ten major Empires from the Mesopotamian valley and central Europe! These Empires invoke their carnal philosophy and religious practices on their captives. These ideologies are swallowed by the nations of the world time after time. Present day wars are of a latent religious nature. Some are more transparent than others. Radical Islam is a popular one these days. There are others less transparent; but all are leading up to a *"new world order"* of *"coexist"* with each other!

Nimrod was the first to war against his neighbors! <u>The Red Horse is the embodiment of humanity in a continual struggle through war to overpower, control, and dominate his fellowman.</u> War, carnage, and bloodshed are common denominator for every tribe and nation of people since Cain slew his brother Able! If evil is a force in the world there will be war! History often is no more than a long list of wars and rumors of wars. Even Jesus comments about this situation; especially in the end times before His return to earth.

Jesus warns that wars and persecutions are not going to end until his second return!

> ***Matthew 24:6-8*** *And ye shall hear of wars and rumors of wars: see that ye be not troubled: for all these things must come to pass, but the end is not yet. (7) For nation, shall rise against nation, and kingdom against kingdom: and there shall be famines, and pestilences, and earthquakes, in different places. (8) All these are the beginning of sorrows.*

I hope you see the parallel once again with what Jesus teaches at the mount of Olives and the first four seals of Revelation.

Christ will judge and make war upon the wicked nations of humanity!

Revelation 19:11-12 *And I saw heaven opened and behold a white horse; and he that sat upon him was called Faithful and True, and in righteousness he doth judge and make war. (12) His eyes were as a flame of fire, and on his head, were many crowns; and he had a name written, that no man knew, but he himself.*

The Second Seal reveals there is ongoing bloodshed and war against one another as religious persecution for carnal reasons of domination and control of the world!

This will continue right up to Armageddon!

THE BLACK HORSE:
The Third Seal Opened
- ➢ The Black Horse is symbolic of famine and pestilence on crops and staple foods for supporting physical life on earth.
- ➢ Balances are symbolic of the extreme scarcity of food and the expense of what is available.

Revelation 6:5-6 *And when he had opened the third seal, I heard the third beast say, See. And I beheld, and lo a black horse; and he that sat on him had a pair of balances in his hand. (6) And I heard a voice in the middle of the four beasts say, a measure of wheat for a penny, and three measures of barley for a penny; and see thou hurt not the oil and the wine.*

From the times of Joseph there have been famines and scarcity of food. What food is available comes with great expense. Even in our modern times, people in parts of the world go to bed hungry every night!

Sadly, this is also true in America! Our restaurants throw away more food than many people in our country ever consume in a week! Third world nations suffer from it too, to the point of death. The Third Seal of the scroll reveals famine, pestilences, and natural disasters upon humanity; a result of abandoning the Faith Once Delivered! Just this morning, the news reports a strain of bacteria infecting humans that threatens the most powerful anti-biotic medicine available to fight it. These pestilences are becoming immune to our bodily defenses and medicines to stop them!

THE PALE HORSE:
The Fourth Seal Opened
- ➢ The Pale Horse is symbolic of the results of all the first three seals depict.
- ➢ Certain death from these events followed by the grave to bury the dead.
- ➢ At least ¼ of the world will be affected by these sorrows and troubles.
- ➢ The military powers of nations will war with each other. (*beasts*)
- ➢ Famine, disease, and pestilence will follow the destructive forces.

Revelation 6:7-8 *And when he had opened the fourth seal, I heard the voice of the fourth beast say, Come and see. (8) And I looked and behold a pale horse: and his name that sat on him was Death, and Hell followed with him. And power was given unto them over the fourth part of the earth, to kill with sword, and with hunger, and with death, and with the beasts of the earth.*

The Fourth Horseman can easily be the "Grim Reaper!" The Fourth Seal stands for death from the many causes of the first three seals and will destroy at least ¼ of the population of the world over a period of wars, famines, and disasters in the later days. The *"black plague"* of medieval times. Bubonic plague, Cholera, Leprosy, Ebola, Typhoid, and as of late the Zika virus are just a few examples of pestilence and biological disorders in the world down through time. These outbreaks of disease cause death. Death from famine and all types of diseases. Heart disease, Cancer, Leukemia, Syphilis, Aids, and Diabetes are all prevalent killers in these modern times!

These **Four Seals** are a brief overview of how these are the result of abandoning the Truth of God's way of life proven and exemplified by Jesus Christ as the way of truth and righteousness! These **Four Horseman** are representation of man's deceit, evil, and corrupt conditions, religions, and governments when obedience to God is not the driving force behind mankind's living life! They are religious and political agendas to dominate masses of people for personal power and aggrandizement, even worship! *(It is carnal humanity turned loose.)*

Prophetically we can parallel these **Four Horsemen** from Revelation 6:2-8 with what Jesus tells His disciples in Matthew 24.

> *Matthew 24:5-8 For many shall **come in my name, saying, I am Christ**; and shall deceive many. (6) And ye shall hear of **wars and rumors of wars**: see that ye be not troubled: for all these things, must come to pass, but the end is not yet. (7) For nation shall rise against nation, and kingdom against kingdom: and there shall be **famines, and pestilences**, and **earthquakes, in different places**. (8) All these are the beginning of sorrows.*

Just since records have been kept there have been no less than nearly One-billion lives lost down through history from major earthquakes and natural disasters! That is one-seventh of today's world population! One can only imagine how many billions of human beings have died since the flood of Noah's time from the *"representations"* of these Four Horsemen!

Jesus warns that things in the world will be in chaos until His return near the end of days. <u>These seals are an overview of events that effect humanity down through time as kingdoms of men are looking to rule the world with false religion and in their own way.</u>

So, the *"stage"* is now set by long years of these predicted events of disaster and deceit for why there will be a Coming Apocalypse!

SUMMARY THUS FAR

As a national phenomenon, these are represented as continuous events down thru the times of History and will remain active until Christ returns.

FIRST SEAL*: WHITE HORSE; Deceit, false teachers, false religions:*
SECOND SEAL*: RED HORSE; Military War Lords, Wars, Religious wars:*
THIRD SEAL*: BLACK HORSE; Diseases, Pestilences, Famine, Poverty, Plagues:*
FOURTH SEAL*: PALE HORSE; Death; The result of mankind's actions:*

HISTORY REPEATS THE DEEDS OF EVIL MEN

History is a record of wars, religious and political, between nations of men for power since the family of Noah left the Ark. The dead bodies are as many as the stars in the night sky. Billions of people have died since the flood of Noah from natural disasters, but mostly from humanity warring among itself for power and domination. The genocide of whole races of people has been tried over and over. The six-million Jews of WWII are a drop in the bucket of millions before them.

At present day, the Syrians are being gassed and murdered systematically by their own leaders and people in power. It is sometimes called *"ethnic cleansing."* What a terrible thing to do to a race of people. Russia is scooping up the leftovers of Syrian misfortune.

There is a source of evil in the world and someday it will affect you and me! The bible says it plainly:

> ***Proverbs 14:12***
> *There is a way which seems right unto a man, but the end thereof are the ways of death.*

CHAPTER SIX

SEALS FIVE, SIX AND SEVEN

The next three seals of the Seven Seals in Revelation are <u>heavenly scenes and future events.</u>

They involve the good and bad people of the earth and what will be their fate during these <u>times of the coming of Jesus Christ</u>. It will take us to the Second Coming of Christ.

> **Revelation 6:9-11**
>
> *(9) And when he had opened the **fifth seal**, I saw under the altar the souls of them that were slain for the word of God, and for the testimony which they held:*

[80]This would be all the martyred believers since the time of Christ up until the 7th Trumpet when the 1st resurrection of the saints takes place at the second coming of Jesus Christ.

---

[80]   *Revelation 6:12*
*(12) And I beheld when he had opened **the sixth seal,** and, lo, <u>there was a great earthquake; and the sun became black as sackcloth of hair, and the moon became as blood;</u>*

> *(10) And they cried with a loud voice, saying,* **How long, O Lord, holy and true, dost thou not judge and avenge our blood on them that dwell on the earth?**
>
> *(11) And white robes were given unto every one of them; and it was said unto them, that they should rest yet for a little season,* **until their fellow servants also and their brethren, that should be killed as they were, should be fulfilled**.

Now remember, **this is a vision**. These people appear to be alive, but in reality John is seeing this in a dream or vision. (Joh 3:13 And no man has ascended to heaven, but he that came down from heaven, *only* the Son of man which is in heaven.)

> *Revelation 14:13*
>
> *(13) And I heard a voice from heaven saying unto me, Write,* **Blessed are the dead which die in the Lord from henceforth**: *Yea, saith the Spirit, that they may rest from their labors; and their works do follow them.*

These are the believers who live and die up to the Second Coming of Christ.

This will include the **144,000** that are sealed by God during the **Great Tribulation** along with an innumerable multitude of believers.

This part of the 5th seal carries over into some "Inset" chapters in Revelation.

> ***Revelation 7:1-4***
>
> *(1) And after these things I saw four angels standing on the four corners of the earth, holding the four winds of the earth, that the wind should not blow on the earth, nor on the sea, nor on any tree.*
>
> *(2) And I saw another angel ascending from the east,* ***having the seal of the living God***: *and he cried with a loud voice to the four angels, to whom it was given to hurt the earth and the sea,*
>
> *(3) Saying, Hurt not the earth, neither the sea, nor the trees,* **till we have sealed the servants of our God in their foreheads.**
>
> *(4) And I heard the number of them which were sealed: and there were sealed an hundred and forty and four thousands of all the tribes of the children of Israel.*

This number could be an arbitrary number depicting that a lot of the Israelites will be sealed and saved during the Great Tribulation. Only God knows that number when the time comes.

Revelation 7:9-17

(9) After this I beheld, and, lo, **a great multitude, which no man could number, of all nations, and kindreds, and people, and tongues,** *stood before the throne, and before the Lamb, clothed with white robes, and palms in their hands;*

(10) And cried with a loud voice, saying, Salvation to our God which sits upon the throne, and unto the Lamb.

(11) And all the angels stood round about the throne, and about the elders and the four beasts, and fell before the throne on their faces, and worshipped God,

(12) Saying, Amen: Blessing, and glory, and wisdom, and thanksgiving, and honor, and power, and might, be unto our God for ever and ever. Amen.

(13) And one of the elders answered, saying unto me, **What are these which are arrayed in white robes? and whence came they?**

(14) And I said unto him, Sir, thou know. And he said to me, **These are they which came out of great tribulation, and have washed their robes, and made them white in the blood of the Lamb.**

(15) Therefore are they before the throne of God, and serve him day and night in his temple: and he that sits on the throne shall dwell among them.

(16) They shall hunger no more, neither thirst anymore; neither shall the sun light on them, nor any heat.

*(17) For the Lamb which is in the midst of the throne shall feed them, and shall lead them unto living fountains of waters: and **God shall wipe away all tears from their eyes.***

The timing is exact, these are those who make it through the Great Tribulation with the supernatural help of God and Jesus Christ!

The **Sixth seal** begins and ends with **the Day of The Lord.**

> ### Revelation 6:12-17
> *(12) And I beheld when he had opened the **sixth seal**, and, lo, there was a great earthquake; and the sun became black as sackcloth of hair, and the moon became as blood;*
>
> *(13) And the stars of heaven fell unto the earth, even as a fig tree casts her untimely figs, when she is shaken of a mighty wind.*
>
> *(14) And the heaven departed as a scroll when it is rolled together; and every mountain and island were moved out of their places.*
>
> *(15) And the kings of the earth, and the great men, and the rich men, and the chief captains, and the mighty men, and every bondman, and every free man, hid themselves in the dens and in the rocks of the mountains;*
>
> *(16) And said to the mountains and rocks, Fall on us, and **hide us from the face of him that sits on the throne, and from the wrath of the Lamb:***
>
> *(17) **For the great day of his wrath is come; and who shall be able to stand?***

There are a lot of "*inset*" scriptures in Revelation that fill in some details down through history. The chapters do not flow one after the other. This is where we must consult other prophesies to fill in the blanks. There are a lot of events that happen before the 5th and 6th seal events take place.

To aid in this process I will box in some the of events leading up to the Second return of Christ. These will not have dates. This is because they are ahead in our future, and we must wait and watch these events develop leading up to the Second coming.

Remember, Prophesies can change. This can get confusing; I will create a Chart outlining the events that are scattered throughout the scriptures.
Possible Events in our near Future

> There will eventually be an Economic decline in America. This could prompt a New World Currency and Economic Situation worldwide that could mean the U.S. dollar is no more the world standard.
> This could speed up the **New World Order** for the nations of the world. This could be the **German led United States of Europe taking charge of world Economics.**

Revelation 13:15-18

*(15) And he had power to give life unto the image of the **beast**, that the image of the beast should both speak, and cause that as many as would not worship the image of the beast should be killed.*

*(16) And he causes all, both small and great, rich and poor, free and bond, to **receive a mark in their right hand, or in their foreheads:***

*(17) **And that no man might buy or sell, save he that had the mark**, or the name of the beast, or the number of his name.*

*(18) Here is wisdom. Let him that hath understanding count the number of the beast: for it is the number of a man; and his number is **Six hundred threescore and six.***

> **The Jews will build a 3rd Temple in Jerusalem**
> The Pope would become instrumental in
> bringing peace to the Middle East.
> The Pope (*at that time*) could move his headquarters to Jerusalem.
> He would then join with the Beast Power to enforce
> the Economic and Political Powers to create a peace
> among the nations that would comply.

> When the **New World Order** is in place, there will
> be **3 ½ Years of peace** and prosperity for those
> who have the mark and worship the beast.
> However, after 3 ½ Years the whole Order will fall apart. <u>The
> Head of the Beast Power will want to be without the influence
> of the Pope or False Prophet and will destroy the relationship.
> The Beast Power would then take over the
> temple and claim himself God.</u>

2Thessalonians 2:4-8

(4) *Who opposes and exalts himself above all that is called God, or that is worshipped; so* **that he as God sits in the temple of God, shewing himself that he is God.**

The Pope already assumes the place of Christ and has recently said that the Catholic Church supersedes the Bible in authority. He will be replaced by the "anti-Christ" Beast Power.

(5) *Remember ye not, that, when I was yet with you, I told you these things?*

(6) *And now ye know what with holds that he might be revealed in his time.*

(7) **For the mystery of iniquity doth already work**: *only he who now let's will let, until he be taken out of the way.*

(8) *And* **then shall that Wicked be revealed,** *whom* **the Lord shall consume with the spirit of his mouth, and shall destroy with the brightness of his coming**:

[81]This "*Wicked One*" is the Beast Leader who kicks the False Prophet out.

Revelation 17:15-17

(15) And he saith unto me, The waters which thou saw, where the whore sits, are peoples, and multitudes, and nations, and tongues.

Total influence over the nations.

*(16) And the **ten horns which thou saw upon the beast**, these shall hate the whore, and shall make her desolate and naked, and shall eat her flesh, and burn her with fire.*

These are the Ten Leaders of the United States of Europe and Common Market who along with the King of the Beast will remove the False Prophet from his position.

(17) For God hath put in their hearts to fulfil his will, and to agree, and give their kingdom unto the beast, until the words of God shall be fulfilled.

The people of the world will give their allegiance to the Beast Power. This will trigger the Great Tribulation.

> **The Great Tribulation** will begin because of the Beast Power demanding dominance over the nations. **This will last another 3 ½ Years**. During this time is when the **Two Witnesses** with make havoc with the Beast Power and cause it to eventually kill the Two Witnesses.

Matthew 24:21-24

*(21) For then shall be **great tribulation**, such as was not since the beginning of the world to this time, no, nor ever shall be.*

(22) And except those days should be shortened, there should no flesh be saved: but for the elect's sake those days shall be shortened.

(23) Then if any man shall say unto you, Lo, here is Christ, or there; believe it not.

---

[81] ***Matthew 24:27***

(27) <u>For as the lightning cometh out of the east, and shineth even unto the west</u>; so shall also the coming of the Son of man be.

*(24) For **there shall arise false Christs, and false prophets, and shall shew great signs and wonders**; insomuch that, **if it were possible, they shall deceive the very elect.***

This is an "INSET" Chapter in Revelation 11: (the last 3 ½ years of Christ's ministry that was cut-off by His crucifixion.

Revelation 11:3-10

*(3) And I will give power unto my **two witnesses**, and they shall prophesy a thousand two hundred and threescore days, clothed in sackcloth.*

(4) These are the two olive trees, and the two candlesticks standing before the God of the earth.

*(5) **And if any man will hurt them**, fire proceeds out of their mouth, and devours their enemies: and if any man will hurt them, he must in this manner be killed.*

*(6) **These have power to shut heaven, that it rain not in the days of their prophecy**: and have **power over waters to turn them to blood, and to smite the earth with all plagues, as often as they will.***

These two witnesses will finish the work that Christ started during His ministry for 3 ½ Years ending in 30 A.D. with His crucifixion.

*(7) And when they shall have finished their testimony, **the beast** that ascends out of the bottomless pit shall make war against them, and **shall overcome them, and kill them.***

(8) And their dead bodies shall lie in the street of the great city, which spiritually is called Sodom and Egypt, where also our Lord was crucified. (Jerusalem)

(9) And they of the people and kindreds and tongues and nations shall see their dead bodies three days and an half, and shall not suffer their dead bodies to be put in graves.

*(10) And they that dwell upon the earth shall rejoice over them, and make merry, and shall send gifts one to another; **because these two prophets** tormented them that dwelt on the earth.*

All of this is leading up to the Battle of Armageddon.
Now back to the **sixth seal** scenario:

Matthew 24:29-31
*(29) **Immediately after the tribulation of those days***
(This is at the end of the Great Tribulation)
⁸²shall the sun be darkened, and the moon shall not give her light, and the stars shall fall from heaven, and the powers of the heavens shall be shaken:
(30) And then shall appear ⁸³the sign of the Son of man in heaven: and then shall all the tribes of the earth mourn, and they shall see the Son of man coming in the clouds of heaven with power and great glory.
(There will be a bright new light in the heavens that the world will see for several days as the Son of God approaches the earth for the Second Coming.)
(31) And Christ shall send His angels with a great sound of a trumpet, and they shall gather together his elect from the four winds, from one end of heaven to the other.

This will be the beginning of the First Resurrection.

Revelation 19:7-10
*(7) Let us be glad and rejoice, and give honorr to him: for **the marriage of the Lamb is come**, and **his wife*** (The Spiritual church of Christ's believers) *hath made herself ready.*
*(8) And to her was granted that she should be arrayed in fine linen, clean and white: **for the fine linen is the righteousness of saints.***

---

[82]   *1Thessalonians 4:13-18*
(13) But I would not have you to be ignorant, brethren, concerning them which are asleep, that ye sorrow not, even as others which have no hope.
(14) For if we believe that Jesus died and rose again, even so them also which sleep in Jesus will God bring with him.
(15) For this we say unto you by the word of the Lord, that we which are alive and remain unto the coming of the Lord shall not prevent them which are asleep.
(16) For the Lord himself shall descend from heaven with a shout, with the voice of the archangel, and with the trump of God: and the dead in Christ shall rise first:
*(17) **Then we which are alive and remain shall be caught up together with them in the clouds, to meet the Lord in the air: and so shall we ever be with the Lord.*** (Marriage Supper of the Lamb)
(18) Wherefore comfort one another with these words.

[83]   Revelation the 9th Chapter

⁸⁴*(9) And he saith unto me, Write,* **Blessed are they which are called unto the marriage supper of the Lamb**. *And he saith unto me, These are the true sayings of God.*

---

84   *Revelation 16:1-16*
(1) And I heard a great voice out of the temple saying to the seven angels, Go your ways, and pour out the vials of the wrath of God upon the earth.
(2) And the first went, and poured out his vial upon the earth; and **there fell a noisome and grievous sore upon the men which had the mark of the beast, and upon them which worshipped his image.**
(3) And the second angel poured out his vial upon the sea; and it became as the blood of a dead man: and every living soul died in the sea.
(4) And the third angel poured out his vial upon the rivers and fountains of waters; and they became blood.
(5) And I heard the angel of the waters say, Thou art righteous, O Lord, which art, and was, and shalt be, because thou hast judged thus.
(6) **For they have shed the blood of saints and prophets, and thou hast given them blood to drink; for they are worthy.**
(7) And I heard another out of the altar say, Even so, Lord God Almighty, true and righteous are thy judgments.
(8) And the fourth angel poured out his vial upon the sun; <u>and power was given unto him to scorch men with fire.</u>
(9) **And men were scorched with great heat, and blasphemed the name of God, which hath power over these plagues: <u>and they repented not to give him glory.</u>**
(10) And the fifth angel poured out his vial upon the seat of the beast; and his kingdom was full of darkness; and they gnawed their tongues for pain,
(11) **And blasphemed the God of heaven because of their pains and their sores<u>, and repented not of their deeds.</u>**
(12) And the sixth angel poured out his vial upon the great river Euphrates; and the water thereof was dried up, that the way of the kings of the east might be prepared.
(13) **And I saw three unclean spirits like frogs come out of the mouth of the dragon, and out of the mouth of the beast, and out of the mouth of the false prophet.**
(14) **For they are the spirits of devils, working miracles, which go forth unto the kings of the earth and of the whole world, to gather them to the battle of that great day of God Almighty.**
(15) Behold, I come as a thief. Blessed is he that watches, and keeps his garments, lest he walk naked, and they see his shame.
(16) **And he gathered them together into a place called in the Hebrew tongue Armageddon.**

*(10) And I fell at his feet to worship him. And he said unto me, See thou do it not: I am thy fellow servant, and of thy brethren that have the testimony of Jesus: worship God: **for the testimony of Jesus is the spirit of prophecy.***

All this scenario will be going on as the people of the Beast will be preparing to fight against the coming light of Christ. They will be convinced Christ is an alien invasion from outer space.

This will be when the **War of Armageddon** will take place in the valley of Megiddo just outside of Jerusalem. Modern Israel and the Valley of Megiddo.

Kibbutz Megiddo is nearby, less than 1 kilometer (0.62 mi) to the south. Today, Megiddo Junction is on the main road connecting the center of Israel with lower Galilee and the north. It lies at the northern entrance to Wadi Ara, an important mountain pass connecting the Jezreel Valley with Israel's coastal plain.

In 1964, during Pope Paul VI's visit to the Holy Land, Megiddo was the site where he met with Israeli dignitaries, including Israeli President Zalman Shazar and Prime Minister Levi Eshkol.

Christians believe that Armageddon will be the site of the final battle between Jesus Christ and the kings of the Earth who go to war against Israel, as outlined in the Book of Revelation.

Back to the book of **Daniel** for some details prior to the Battle of Armageddon. These details involve the Beast Power Leader after he has abandoned the False Prophet and set himself up as God. Following scriptures are another *"snapshot"* of conditions during the Great Tribulation. Its focus is on the Beast Power that sits in the temple. (King of the North)

Daniel 11:31-45

(31) And arms shall stand on his part, and they shall pollute the sanctuary of strength, and shall take away the daily sacrifice, and they shall place the abomination that makes desolate.

Nothing more abominable than a man sitting in a holy temple claiming to be God.

(32) And such as do wickedly against the covenant shall he corrupt by flatteries: but the people that do know their God shall be strong, and do exploits.

Some will take the "mark" and fall prey to the Beast Power. Yet some will be strong and defend their belief in Jesus to the end.

(33) And they that understand among the people shall instruct many: yet they shall fall by the sword, and by flame, by captivity, and by spoil, many days.

This will go on for at least 3 ½ Years.

(34) Now when they shall fall, they shall be holpen with a little help: but many shall cleave to them with flatteries.

(35) And some of them of understanding shall fall, to try them, and to purge, and to make them white, even to the time of the end: because it is yet for a time appointed.

Some believers will have their faith tested to insure they will be in the 1st resurrection.

(36) And the king shall do according to his will; and he shall exalt himself, and magnify himself above every god, and shall speak marvelous things against the God of gods, and shall prosper till the indignation be accomplished: for that that is determined shall be done.

(37) **Neither shall he regard the God of his fathers,** (probable reference to the ancient god of Assyrians, Assur. Speculation on my part) **nor the desire of women, nor regard any god: for he shall magnify himself.**

(38) But in his estate shall he honor the God of forces: and a god whom his father's knew not shall he honor with gold, and silver, and with precious stones, and pleasant things.

(39) Thus shall he do in the most strong holds with a strange god, whom he shall acknowledge and increase with glory: and he shall cause them to rule over many, and shall divide the land for gain.

(40) And at the time of the end shall the king of the south push at him: and the king of the north shall come against him like a whirlwind, with chariots, and with horsemen, and with many ships; and he shall enter into the countries, and shall overflow and pass over.

(41) He shall enter also into the glorious land, and many countries shall be overthrown: but these shall escape out of his hand, even Edom, and Moab, and the chief of the children of Ammon.

(42) He shall stretch forth his hand also upon the countries: and the land of Egypt shall not escape.

(43) But he shall have power over the treasures of gold and of silver, and over all the precious things of Egypt: and the Libyans and the Ethiopians shall be at his steps.

The Beast will conquer the Arab world and others to take their treasures and freedom.

*(44) But **tidings out of the east** and **out of the north shall trouble him**: therefore he shall go forth with great fury to destroy, and utterly to make away many.*

Russia and China will come into the valley of Megiddo and war with the beast and the coming Christ. The Battle of Armageddon!

(45) And he shall plant the tabernacles of his palace between the seas in the glorious holy mountain; yet he shall come to his end, and none shall help him.

There is another description of this **Armageddon** in the book of Revelation.

[85]I listed a reference in the footnotes. This is part of the battle of Armageddon including the plagues from God upon the wicked men of the Beast Power. Notice they do not repent and still are fighting against Jesus when He returns.

Another heavenly scene about the Battle of Armageddon:

Revelation 14:14-20

(14) And I looked, and behold a white cloud, and upon the cloud one sat like unto the Son of man, having on his head a golden crown, and in his hand a sharp sickle.

Jesus Christ coming with power.

(15) And another angel came out of the temple, crying with a loud voice to him that sat on the cloud, Thrust in thy sickle, and reap: for the time is come for thee to reap; for the harvest of the earth is ripe.

(16) And he that sat on the cloud thrust in his sickle on the earth; and the earth was reaped.

---

[85] *Revelation 18:1-24*

These two verses are a reference to the 1st Resurrection of the Saints.

(17) And another angel came out of the temple which is in heaven, he also having a sharp sickle.

(18) And another angel came out from the altar, which had power over fire; and cried with a loud cry to him that had the sharp sickle, saying, Thrust in thy sharp sickle, and gather the clusters of the vine of the earth; for her grapes are fully ripe.

(19) And the angel thrust in his sickle into the earth, and gathered the vine of the earth,

(The wicked who did not bear fruit) *and cast it into the great winepress of the wrath of God.*

(20) And the winepress was trodden without the city, and blood came out of the winepress, even unto the horse bridles, by the space of a thousand and six hundred furlongs.

[86]**Six bowls** of the wrath of God poured out on the wicked and Beast power. They still do not submit to Christ. Read footnote.

The **seventh bowl** of wrath from God.

Revelation 16:17-21

(17) And the seventh angel poured out his vial into the air; and there came a great voice out of the temple of heaven, from the throne, saying, **It is done.**

The final blow from Christ to end the rule of the Kingdoms of men.

---

[86] *Revelation 20:12-15*

(12) And I saw the dead, small and great, stand before God; and the books were opened: and another book was opened, which is the book of life: and the dead were judged out of those things which were written in the books, according to their works.

(13) And the sea gave up the dead which were in it; and death and hell delivered up the dead which were in them: and **they were judged every man according to their works.**

(14) And death and hell were cast into the lake of fire. **This is the second death.**

(15) And **whosoever was not found written in the book of life was cast into the lake of fire.**

*(18) And there were voices, and thunders, and lightnings; and **there was a great earthquake, such as was not since men were upon the earth, so mighty an earthquake, and so great.***

*(19) And the great city was divided into three parts, and the cities of the nation's fell: and great **Babylon came in remembrance before God, to give unto her the cup of the wine of the fierceness of his wrath.***

(20) And every island fled away, and the mountains were not found.

A huge tsunami like no person ever lived through.

[87]*(21) **And there fell upon men a great hail out of heaven, every stone about the weight of a talent: and men blasphemed God because of the plague of the hail; for the plague thereof was exceeding great.***

Note: There is a scripture in Daniel that I think alludes to the time of preparation for the War of Armageddon when Jesus and the saints, (hopefully most of us) will take place. This complete chapter is worth reading as it gives us some detailed information about why there are seals to be opened at the end time.

Daniel 12:1-13

*(1) And at that time shall Michael stand up, the great prince which stands for **the children of thy people**: and **there shall be a time of trouble, such as never was since there was a nation even to that same time: and at that time thy people shall be delivered, every one that shall be found written in the book.***

---

[87] ***Revelation 11:11-13***

(11) And after three days and an half the Spirit of life from God entered into them, and they stood upon their feet; and great fear fell upon them which saw them.

(12) And they heard a great voice from heaven saying unto them, Come up hither. And they ascended up to heaven in a cloud; and their enemies beheld them.

(13) And the same hour was there a great earthquake, and the tenth part of the city fell, and in the earthquake were slain of men seven thousand: and the remnant were affrighted, and gave glory to the God of heaven.

[88]Here we see the importance of being a believer and follower of Jesus Christ. As I explained in my first book, **Why You Were Born**, there are Two Books that God keeps records of all humans born on earth, since the time of Adam. The "Book of Works" and "Book of Life."

(2) And many of them that sleep in the dust of the earth shall awake, some to everlasting life, and some to shame and everlasting contempt.

(3) And they that be wise shall shine as the brightness of the firmament; and they that turn many to righteousness as the stars for ever and ever.

*(4) But thou, O Daniel, shut up the words, and seal the book, even to the time of the end: many shall run to and fro, and **knowledge shall be increased**.*

(5) Then I Daniel looked, and, behold, there stood other two, the one on this side of the bank of the river, and the other on that side of the bank of the river.

*(6) And one said to the man clothed in linen, which was upon the waters of the river, **How long shall it be to the end of these wonders?***

*(7) And I heard the man clothed in linen, which was upon the waters of the river, when he held up his right hand and his left hand unto heaven, and swore by him that lives forever that it shall be **for a time, times, and an half; and when he shall have accomplished to scatter the power of the holy people, all these things shall be finished.*** (This is 3 ½ Years Prophetic: 1260 Days)

(8) And I heard, but I understood not: then said I, O my Lord, what shall be the end of these things?

*(9) And he said, Go thy way, Daniel: **for the words are closed up and sealed till the time of the end.*** (We are living in the time of the end)

*(10) Many shall be purified, and made white, and tried; but the wicked shall do wickedly: and none of the wicked shall understand; but **the wise shall understand**.*

---

[88] *Zechariah 14:1-3*

(1) Behold, the day of the LORD cometh, and thy spoil shall be divided in the midst of thee. (2) For I will gather all nations against Jerusalem to battle; and the city shall be taken, and the houses rifled, and the women ravished; and half of the city shall go forth into captivity, and the residue of the people shall not be cut off from the city.(3) Then shall the LORD go forth, and fight against those nations, as when he fought in the day of battle.

(11) And from the time that the daily sacrifice shall be taken away, and **the abomination that makes desolate set up**, *there shall be* **a thousand two hundred and ninety days.**

(I believe this to be when the False Prophet is kicked out, religious traditions are forbidden, and the Beast Power Leader sets himself up in the Temple)

(12) Blessed is he that waits, and cometh to **the thousand three hundred and five and thirty days.**

(This could be the time of the Marriage Supper of the Lamb with the "first responder saints" newly resurrected and meeting Christ in the air at the banquet table, getting final instructions for coming back to earth for the Battle of Armageddon and establish Christ's kingdom for the next thousand years)

(13) But go thou thy way till the end be: for thou shalt rest, and stand in thy lot at the end of the days. (Daniel will be in the First Resurrection)

Of course, all of this is just speculation on my part, but scripture sure makes it a scenario.

I will create some Charts to help keep the order of things in a timeline perspective.

THE NEW WORLD ORDER, ARMAGEDDON, AND BEYOND

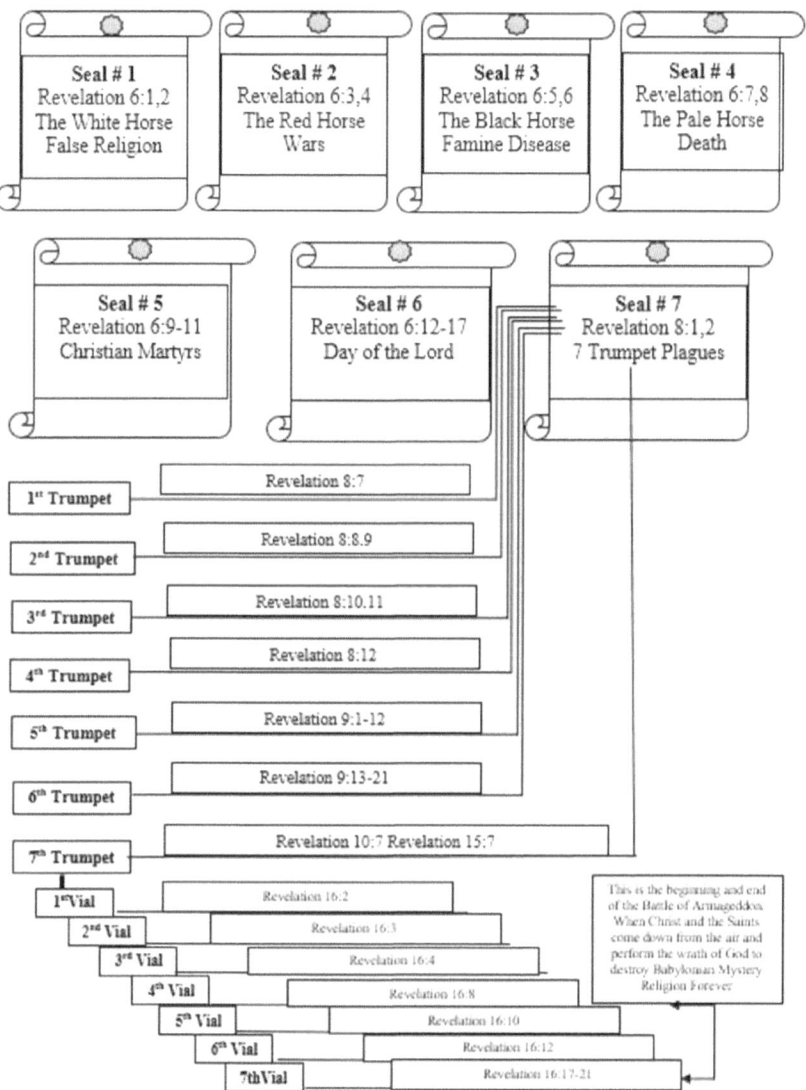

Flow Chart of Events of The Great Tribulation
THE BEGINNING OF THE GREAT TRIBULATION FOR 3 ½ YEARS

- ➤ The Beast will root out the False Prophet = Revelation 17:16
- ➤ This will begin the Great Tribulation on Earth = Matthew 24:21,22
- ➤ The Beast will take over the Temple in Jerusalem and proclaim himself God. = 2Thessalonians 2:4
- ➤ No one worldwide can buy or sell without the MARK of the BEAST = Revelation 13:16,17
- ➤ The Beast Power will make war with the King of the South = Daniel 11:40

EVENTS DURING THE GREAT TRIBULATION FOR 3 ½ YEARS

- ➤ The Two Witnesses will come to Jerusalem to minister = Revelation 11:1-6
- ➤ The sealing of the 144,00 of the tribes of Israel by God = Revelation 7:4
- ➤ Many Christians will remain faithful and give their lives to Christ = Revelation 7:9-17
- ➤ The 7th Seal with 7 Trumpet plagues 4 will sound more to come = Revelation 8:1-13
- ➤ The last 3 Trumpets are the 3 Woes. 5th Trumpet is warfare among the nations = Revelation 9:1-12
- ➤ The 6th Trumpet, 2nd Woe, an army of 2 million will meet in Megiddo = Revelation 9:13-21

THE LAST PART OF THE GREAT TRIBULATION AND ITS END

- ➢ The Two Witnesses will be slain in the streets of Jerusalem, dead for 3 ½ days = Revelation 11:7-10
- ➢ The Two Witnesses come to life and a voice from heaven calls them up = Revelation 11:11-14
- ➢ The 7th trumpet sounds, and the nations were angry ready to fight = Revelation 11:15-19
- ➢ With the sounding of the 7th trumpet Christ begins to rule, the 1st Resurrection = Revelation 10:7
- ➢ The dead in Christ rise and those who are alive are changed = 1 Corinthians 15:50-57
- ➢ All the risen saints will meet with Christ in the Air = 1 Thessalonians 4:13-18
- ➢ Marriage Supper of Christ, preparing for the Battle of Armageddon = Revelation 19:7-9
- ➢ Jesus and the Saints will appear at Armageddon for the War to end War = Revelation 19:11-21/Jude 1:14,15

CHAPTER SEVEN

ARMAGEDDON AND THE KINGDOM OF GOD

Revelation 16:16
*(16) And he gathered them together **into a place called in the Hebrew tongue Armageddon**.*

The Battle of Armageddon will happen when Jesus Christ and the resurrected saints return from the Marriage Supper of the Lamb to earth. I will pick up the timeline in the book of Thessalonians. This passage of scripture is especially important to every person who believes or thinks they want to believe in the saving power of Jesus Christ. It is the ultimate hope for us as Christians. [89]This event will happen just before the 7th Trumpet sounds. The two witnesses, who were dead in the streets of Jerusalem for 3.5 days will be told to *"come up here."*

> *Revelation 11:15*
> *(15) And the **seventh angel sounded**; and there were great voices in heaven, saying, **The kingdoms of this world are become the kingdoms of our Lord, and of his Christ; and he shall reign for ever and ever.***

---

[89] *2Thessalonians 2:8*
*(8) And then shall that **Wicked be revealed**, whom the Lord shall consume with the spirit of his mouth, and shall destroy with the brightness of his coming:*

1Thessalonians 4:13-18

(13) But I would not have you to be ignorant, brethren, concerning **them** *which are asleep, that ye sorrow not, even as others which have no hope.* (Paul is speaking of those who have died while believing in and serving Jesus Christ.)

(14) For if we believe that Jesus died and rose again, even so **them** *also which sleep in Jesus will* **God bring with him**. (This is specific information as to who them are)

(15) For this we say unto you by the word of the Lord, that **we which are alive and remain unto the coming of the Lord** *shall not precede* **them** *which are asleep.*

(16) For the Lord himself shall descend from heaven with a shout, with the voice of the archangel, and with the trump of God: and **the dead in Christ shall rise first***:*

(17) Then **we which are alive and remain shall be caught up together with them in the clouds, to meet the Lord in the air***:*

> (We will meet Jesus in the atmosphere of earth and then be seated at the marriage supper of the Lamb) *and so shall we ever be with the Lord.* (The bible interprets itself)

(18) Wherefore comfort one another with these words.

Revelation 19:6-9

(6) And I heard as it were the voice of a great multitude, and as the voice of many waters, and as the voice of mighty thundering, saying, Alleluia: for the Lord God omnipotent reigns.

(7) Let us be glad and rejoice, and give honor to him: for the marriage of the Lamb is come, and his wife hath made herself ready.

(8) And to her was granted that she should be arrayed in fine linen, clean and white: for the fine linen is the righteousness of saints.

(9) And he saith unto me, Write, **Blessed are they which are called unto the marriage supper of the Lamb. And he saith unto me, These are the true sayings of God.**

Notice the next scripture about the people on earth when they see Jesus coming.

Revelation 11:18

*(18) **And the nations were angry**, and thy wrath is come, and the time of the dead, that they should be judged, and that thou shouldest give reward unto thy servants the prophets, and to the saints, and them that fear thy name, small and great; and shouldest destroy them which destroy the earth.*

It is hard for me to believe that there are people that are so selfish and hardheaded that they still reject Christ after all the plagues and troubles of the Great Tribulation. Read the next chapter about the vials of wrath that Christ has the angels pour out on these wicked people. It is unbelievable how they respond.

Revelation 16:1-14

*(1) And I heard a great voice out of the temple saying to the seven angels, **Go your ways, and pour out the vials of the wrath of God upon the earth.***

*(2) And the **first** went, and poured out his vial upon the earth; and there fell a noisome and grievous sore upon the men which had the mark of the beast, and upon them which worshipped his image.*

*(3) And the **second angel poured out his vial** upon the sea; and it became as the blood of a dead man: and every living soul died in the sea.*

*(4) And the **third angel poured out his vial** upon the rivers and fountains of waters; and they became blood.*

(5) And I heard the angel of the waters say, Thou art righteous, O Lord, which art, and wast, and shalt be, because thou hast judged thus.

(6) For they have shed the blood of saints and prophets, and thou hast given them blood to drink; for they are worthy.

(7) And I heard another out of the altar say, Even so, Lord God Almighty, true and righteous are thy judgments.

*(8) And the **fourth angel poured out his vial** upon the sun; and power was given unto him to scorch men with fire.*

(9) And men were scorched with great heat, and blasphemed the name of God, which hath power over these plagues: and they repented not to give him glory.

*(10) And the **fifth angel poured out his vial** upon the seat of the beast; and his kingdom was full of darkness; and they gnawed their tongues for pain,*

(11) And blasphemed the God of heaven because of their pains and their sores, and repented not of their deeds.

*(12) And the **sixth angel poured out his vial upon** the great river Euphrates; and the water thereof was dried up, that the way of the kings of the east might be prepared.*

*(13) And I **saw three unclean spirits** like frogs **come out of the mouth of the dragon**, and **out of the mouth of the beast**, and **out of the mouth of the false prophet**.*

*(14) **For they are the spirits of devils**, working miracles, which go forth unto the kings of the earth and of the whole world, to gather them to the battle of that great day of God Almighty.*

Evil spirits deceiving the people with their miracles and wonders.

The seventh and last vial is poured out and yet these wicked armies of men are ready to fight in the Battle of Armageddon.

Revelation 16:17-21

*(17) And the **seventh angel poured out his vial into the air**; and there came a great voice out of the temple of heaven, from the throne, saying, **It is done**.*

*(18) And there were voices, and thunders, and lightnings; and there was **a great earthquake, such as was not since men were upon the earth**, so mighty an earthquake, and so great.*

*(19) And the **great city was divided into three parts**, and **the cities of the nation's fell**: and great Babylon came in remembrance before God, to give unto her the cup of the wine of the fierceness of his wrath.*

(20) And every island fled away, and the mountains were not found.

*(21) **And there fell upon men a great hail out of heaven**, every stone about the weight of a talent: **and men blasphemed God because of the plague of the hail**; for the plague thereof was exceeding great.*

Notice, they don't repent, they curse God for their punishment.

Next scripture tells us the number of the army that fights against Christ and the saints.

Revelation 9:16-21

*(16) And the number of the army of the horsemen were **two hundred thousand thousand**: and I heard the number of them.*

(17) And thus I saw the horses in the vision, and them that sat on them, having breastplates of fire, and of jacinth, and brimstone: and the heads of the horses were as the heads of lions; and out of their mouths issued fire and smoke and brimstone.

(18) By these three was the third part of men killed, by the fire, and by the smoke, and by the brimstone, which issued out of their mouths. (Modern weapons that John found hard to describe)

(19) For their power is in their mouth, and in their tails: for their tails were like unto serpents, and had heads, and with them they do hurt. (Modern weapons that John found hard to describe)

(20) And the rest of the men which were not killed by these plagues **yet repented not of the works of their hands, that they should not worship devils, and idols of gold, and silver, and brass, and stone, and of wood: which neither can see, nor hear, nor walk:**

(21) **Neither repented they of their murders, nor of their sorceries, nor of their fornication, nor of their thefts.**

Incorrigible wicked people!

THE SECOND RETURN OF JESUS CHRIST

Revelation 19:11-21

(11) [90] And I saw heaven opened, and behold a white horse; and He that sat upon him was called Faithful and True, and in righteousness doth judge and make war.

(12) His eyes were as a flame of fire, and on his head were many crowns; and he had a name written, that no man knew, but He Hhimself.

(13) And he was clothed with a vesture dipped in blood: and his name is called **The Word of God.**

(14) And the **armies which were in heaven followed Him upon white horses, clothed in fine linen, white and clean.** *(*These are the saints from the 1ˢᵗ resurrection*)*

---

[90] ***Malachi 4:1***

(1) For, behold, the day cometh, that shall burn as an oven; and all the proud, yea, and ***all that do wickedly****, shall be stubble: and* ***the day that cometh shall burn them up****, saith the LORD of hosts,* ***that it shall leave them neither root nor branch.***

(15) And out of His mouth goes a sharp sword, that with it He should smite the nations: and he shall rule them with a rod of iron: and he treads the winepress of the fierceness and wrath of Almighty God.

(16) And his hath on his vesture and on his thigh a name written, **KING OF KINGS, AND LORD OF LORDS.**

(17) And I saw an angel standing in the sun; and he cried with a loud voice, saying to all the fowls that fly in the midst of heaven, **Come and gather yourselves together unto the supper of the great God;** (Armageddon)

(18) **That ye may eat the flesh of kings, and the flesh of captains, and the flesh of mighty men, and the flesh of horses, and of them that sit on them, and the flesh of all men, both free and bond, both small and great.**

(19) And I saw the beast, and the kings of the earth, and their armies, gathered together to make war against him that sat on the horse, and against his army.

(20) [91] *And the beast was taken, and with him the false prophet that wrought miracles before him, with which he deceived them that had received the mark of the beast, and them that worshipped his image. These both were cast alive into a lake of fire burning with brimstone.*

(One can only imagine what type of nuclear weapons will be used causing fire and great heat)

(21) [92] *And the remnant were slain with the sword of Him that sat upon the horse, which sword proceeded out of his mouth: and all the fowls were filled with their flesh.*

Revelation 14:17-20

---

[91] *Matthew 28:18-20*

(18) And Jesus came and spake unto them, saying, All power is given unto me in heaven and in earth.

(19) Go ye therefore, and teach all nations, baptizing them in the name of the Father, and of the Son, and of the Holy Spirit:

(20) Teaching them to observe all things whatsoever I have commanded you: and, lo, I am with you always, even unto the end of the world. Amen.

[92] **Luke 10:20**

(20) Notwithstanding in this rejoice not, that the spirits are subject unto you; but rather **rejoice, because your names are written in heaven.**

(17) And another angel came out of the temple which is in heaven, he also having a sharp sickle.

(18) And another angel came out from the altar, which had power over fire; and cried with a loud cry to him that had the sharp sickle, saying, Thrust in thy sharp sickle, and gather the clusters of the vine of the earth; for her grapes are fully ripe.

(19) And the angel thrust in his sickle into the earth, and gathered the vine of the earth, **and cast it into the great winepress of the wrath of God.**

(20) And the winepress was trodden without the city, and **blood came out of the winepress, even unto the horse bridles, by the space of a thousand and six hundred furlongs**. (That is a path of blood 200 miles long)

END OF THE BATTLE OF ARMAGEDDON

NOTE: The **14th chapter of Zachariah** is a good summary of the end time battle and establishment of Christ's kingdom on earth. Including some geography changes to the landscape around Jerusalem.

Coming Day of the Lord

Zec 14:1 Behold, the day of the LORD cometh, and thy spoil shall be divided in the midst of thee.

Zec 14:2 For I will gather all nations against Jerusalem to battle; and the city shall be taken, and the houses rifled, and the women ravished; and half of the city shall go forth into captivity, and the residue of the people shall not be cut off from the city. ***(This is the prophecy of the Battle of Armageddon)***

Zec 14:3 Then shall the LORD go forth, and fight against those nations, as when he fought in the day of battle.

Zec 14:4 And his feet shall stand in that day upon the mount of Olives, which *is* before Jerusalem on the east, and the mount of Olives shall cleave in the midst thereof toward the east and toward the west, *and there shall be* a very great valley; and half of the mountain shall remove toward the north, and half of it toward the south. ***(Christ will come and cause the Mount of Olives to break into two halves sliding East and West)***

Zec 14:5 And ye shall flee *to* the valley of the mountains; for the valley of the mountains shall reach unto Azal: yea, ye shall flee, like as ye fled from before the earthquake in the days of Uzziah king of Judah: and the LORD my God shall come, *and* **all the saints with thee**. *(Christ will bring the First Responders or First Fruits of the First Resurrection with Him from the Great Supper of the Lamb)*

Zec 14:6 And it shall come to pass in that day, *that* the light shall not be clear, *nor* dark: *(The sun will shine continuous upon Jerusalem)*

Zec 14:7 But it shall be one day which shall be known to the LORD, not day, nor night: but it shall come to pass, *that* at evening time it shall be light.*(the Earth will stop rotation and there will be no night)*

Zec 14:8 And it shall be in that day, *that* living waters shall go out from Jerusalem; half of them toward the former sea, and half of them toward the hinder sea: in summer and in winter shall it be. *(A river will spring from the mount of Olives both directions, North and South to the seas.)*

Zec 14:9 And the LORD shall be king over all the earth: in that day shall there be one LORD, and his name one.

Zec 14:10 All the land shall be turned as a plain from Geba to Rimmon south of Jerusalem: and it shall be lifted up, and inhabited in her place, from Benjamin's gate unto the place of the first gate, unto the corner gate, and *from* the tower of Hananeel unto the king's winepresses.

Zec 14:11 And *men* shall dwell in it, and there shall be no more utter destruction; but Jerusalem shall be safely inhabited. *(There will be physical humans living on the earth, many who survived the Great Tribulation)*

Zec 14:12 And this shall be the plague wherewith the LORD will smite all the people that have fought against Jerusalem; Their flesh shall consume away while they stand upon their feet, and their eyes shall consume away in their holes, and their tongue shall consume away in their mouth. *(This is how the enemies of Christ will die in Armageddon)*

Zec 14:13 And it shall come to pass in that day, *that* a great tumult from the LORD shall be among them; and they shall lay hold everyone on the hand of his neighbor, and his hand shall rise up against the hand of his neighbor.

Zec 14:14 And Judah also shall fight at Jerusalem; and the wealth of all the heathen round about shall be gathered together, gold, and silver, and apparel, in great abundance.

Zec 14:15 And so shall be the plague of the horse, of the mule, of the camel, and of the ass, and of all the beasts that shall be in these tents, as this plague.

Zec 14:16 And it shall come to pass, *that* every one that is left of all the nations which came against Jerusalem shall even go up from year to year to worship the King, the LORD of hosts, and to keep the feast of tabernacles. **(Christ will begin an educational plan for the earth humans to learn about God's ways and means for life)**

Zec 14:17 And it shall be, *that* whoso will not come up of *all* the families of the earth unto Jerusalem to worship the King, the LORD of hosts, even upon them shall be no rain.

Zec 14:18 And if the family of Egypt go not up, and come not, that *have* no *rain;* there shall be the plague, wherewith the LORD will smite the heathen that come not up to keep the feast of tabernacles.

Zec 14:19 This shall be the punishment of Egypt, and the punishment of all nations that come not up to keep the feast of tabernacles. **(Those who do not fall into line will be punished if they do not obey the commanded worship of Hoy Festivals)**

Zec 14:20 In that day shall there be upon the bells of the horses, HOLINESS UNTO THE LORD; and the pots in the LORD'S house shall be like the bowls before the altar.

Zec 14:21 Yea, every pot in Jerusalem and in Judah shall be holiness unto the LORD of hosts: and all they that sacrifice shall come and take of them, and seethe therein: and in that day there shall be no more the Canaanite in the house of the LORD of hosts. **(There will be no more rebellion allowed in the Kingdom of Christ when it is established)**

SATAN BOUND FOR 1, 000 YEARS

Revelation 20:1-3

(1) And I saw an angel come down from heaven, **having the key of the bottomless pit and a great chain in his hand.**

*(2) **And he laid hold on the dragon, that old serpent, which is the Devil, and Satan, and bound him a thousand years,***

*(3) And cast him into the bottomless pit, and shut him up, and set a seal upon him, that he should deceive the nations no more, till the thousand years should be fulfilled: and **after that he must be loosed a little season.*** (This little season will be a future time after the 1,000 years)

- 3.5 Years of Great Tribulation
- Two Witnesses will complete Christ's ministry.
- Two Witnesses killed and then after 3.5 days resurrected.
- God's wrath of vials poured out on the nations.
- Army of 200 million gather at Armageddon.
- 1st Resurrection of the Saints will occur, dead in Christ rise first, others changed.
- Marriage Supper of Christ in the air the Saints will meet Christ.
- Christ and the Saints will return to earth to battle the nations at Armageddon.
- Beast and False Prophet cast into the lake of fire created in the Valley of Armageddon
- Satan will be bound for the next 1,000 years during the reign of Christ and the Saints
- Restoration of the nations of the earth will begin under the leadership of Christ and Saints

Christ's New World Order

It is hard to imagine a world without strife and conflict somewhere. But this will be the time of peace that the world has not known since Cain slew Able. Jesus Christ, King of the planet with thousands of literally *"born again"* spirit beings serving Him and the world of humans that have survived the wrath of God on the nations of the earth. This is the time when prophetic scriptures will be fulfilled. Let's highlight a few of them.

The Apostle Paul explains it well:

1Corinthians 15:50-58

(50) Now this I say, brethren, that flesh and blood cannot inherit the kingdom of God; neither doth corruption inherit incorruption.

(51) Behold, I shew you a mystery; We shall not all sleep, but we shall all be changed,

(52) In a moment, in the twinkling of an eye, at the last trump: for the trumpet shall sound, and the dead shall be raised incorruptible, and we shall be changed.

(53) For this corruptible must put on incorruption, and this mortal *must* put on immortality.

(54) So when this corruptible shall have put on incorruption, and this mortal shall have put on immortality, then shall be brought to pass the saying that is written, Death is swallowed up in victory.

(55) O death, where *is* thy sting? O grave, where *is* thy victory?

(56) The sting of death *is* sin; and the strength of sin *is* the law.

(57) But thanks *be* to God, which giveth us the victory through our Lord Jesus Christ.

(58) Therefore, my beloved brethren, be ye steadfast, unmovable, always abounding in the work of the Lord, forasmuch as ye know that your labor is not in vain in the Lord.

> **1Thessalonians 4:13-17**
>
> (13) But I would not have you to be ignorant, brethren, concerning them which are asleep, that ye sorrow not, even as others which have no hope.
>
> (14) For if we believe that Jesus died and rose again, even so them also which sleep in Jesus will God bring with him.
>
> (15) For this we say unto you by the word of the Lord, that we which are alive *and* remain unto the coming of the Lord shall not prevent them which are asleep.
>
> (16) For the Lord himself shall descend from heaven with a shout, with the voice of the archangel, and with the trump of God: and the dead in Christ shall rise first:
>
> (17) Then we which are alive *and* remain shall be caught up together with them in the clouds, to meet the Lord in the air: and so shall we ever be with the Lord.

These scriptures that we have read for years will be the reality when we reach this time in the future. I wish to insert more scriptures for you to ponder about the "good news" of the Kingdom of God.

We will be Kings and Priests in the Kingdom of God on this earth! I realize this is not the message of 'heaven or hell' that has been promoted for centuries. The bible supports the Kingdom of God established upon this earth. Since the creation of humankind, God has valued the earth and his created physical beings as the center of His plan for expanding the "Spiritual family of God." Jesus Christ is the **firstborn** son of God. He has pioneered the way for all who believe in Him to have the same opportunity for an eternal existence with Him and God the Father. This is our intended destiny as physical human beings.

Matthew 6:9-10

(9) After this manner therefore pray ye: Our Father which art in heaven, Hallowed be thy name.

(10) Thy kingdom come. **Thy will be done in earth**, as *it is* in heaven.

Matthew 6:33

(33) But **seek ye first the kingdom of God**, and his righteousness; and all these things shall be added unto you.

Revelation 1:6

(6) And hath **made us kings and priests unto God and his Father;** to him *be* glory and dominion for ever and ever. Amen.

Revelation 5:10

(10) And **hast made us unto our God kings and priests: and we shall reign on the earth.**

Revelation 20:4

(4) And I saw thrones, and they sat upon them, and judgment was given unto them: and *I saw* the souls of them that were beheaded for the witness of Jesus, and for the word of God, and which had not worshipped the beast, neither his image, neither had received *his* mark upon their foreheads, or in their hands; and **they lived and reigned with Christ a thousand years.**

Revelation 20:6

(6) Blessed and holy *is* he that hath part in the **first resurrection**: on such the second death hath no power, but **they shall be priests of God and of Christ, and shall reign with him a thousand years.**

This is amazing opportunity for us. We will have power to make judgments and rule the nations under the direction of Jesus Christ for a 1,000 Years. This will be a glorious time of restoration. There are other scriptures that confirm what it will be like.

Isaiah 58:12

(12) And *they that shall be* of thee shall build the old waste places: thou shalt raise up the foundations of many generations; **and thou shalt be called, The repairer of the breach, The restorer of paths to dwell in.**

We will be known among the physical humans as the priests of the Lord.

Ezekiel 36:33-35

(33) Thus saith the Lord GOD; In the day that I shall have cleansed you from all your iniquities I will also cause *you* to dwell in the cities, and the wastes shall be built.

(34) And the desolate land shall be tilled, whereas it lay desolate in the sight of all that passed by.

(35) And they shall say, This land that was desolate is become like the garden of Eden; and the waste and desolate and ruined cities *are become* fenced, *and* are inhabited.

These next verses refer to Jesus Christ during this time. Even the wild animals will take on a gentle character and manner. Lions will eat straw like an ox.

Isaiah 11:1-10

(1) And there shall come forth a rod out of the stem of Jesse, and a Branch shall grow out of his roots:

(2) And **the spirit of the LORD shall rest upon Him**,(Jesus) the spirit of wisdom and understanding, the spirit of counsel and might, the spirit of knowledge and of the fear of the LORD;

(3) And shall make Him of quick understanding in the fear of the LORD: and shall not judge after the sight of his eyes, neither reprove after the hearing of his ears:

(4) But with righteousness shall he judge the poor, and reprove with equity for the meek of the earth: and he shall smite the earth with the rod of his mouth, and with the breath of lips shall he slay the wicked.

(5) And righteousness shall be the girdle of his loins, and faithfulness the girdle of his reins.

(6) The wolf also shall dwell with the lamb, and the leopard shall lie down with the kid; and the calf and the young lion and the fatling together; **and a little child shall lead them.**

(7) And the cow and the bear shall feed; their young ones shall lie down together: and the lion shall eat straw like the ox.

(8) And the sucking child shall play on the hole of the asp, and the weaned child shall put his hand on the cockatrice' den.

(9) **They shall not hurt nor destroy in all my holy mountain**: (*metaphor for Kingdom*) for **the earth shall be full of the knowledge of the LORD, as the waters cover the sea.**

(10) And in that day there shall be a root of Jesse, which shall stand for an ensign of the people; to it shall the Gentiles seek: and **His rest shall be glorious.**

A restoring of the nations from all the tribulation days prior to the Kingdom of God.

> **Isaiah 35:1-10**
>
> (1) The wilderness and the solitary place shall be glad for them; and the desert shall rejoice, and blossom as the rose.
>
> (2) It shall blossom abundantly, and rejoice even with joy and singing: the glory of Lebanon shall be given unto it, the excellency of Carmel and Sharon, they shall see the glory of the LORD, *and* the excellency of our God.
>
> (3) Strengthen ye the weak hands, and confirm the feeble knees.
>
> (4) Say to them *that are* of a fearful heart, Be strong, fear not: behold, your God will come *with* vengeance, *even* God *with* a recompence; he will come and save you.
>
> (5) Then the eyes of the blind shall be opened, and the ears of the deaf shall be unstopped.
>
> (6) Then shall the lame *man* leap as an hart, and the tongue of the dumb sing: for in the wilderness shall waters break out, and streams in the desert.
>
> (7) And the parched ground shall become a pool, and the thirsty land springs of water: in the habitation of dragons, where each lay, *shall be* grass with reeds and rushes.
>
> (8) **And an highway shall be there, and a way, and it shall be called The way of holiness**; the unclean shall not pass over it; but it *shall be* for those: the wayfaring men, though fools, shall not err *therein*.
>
> (9) No lion shall be there, nor *any* ravenous beast shall go up there on, it shall not be found there; but **the redeemed shall walk there:**
>
> (10) **And the ransomed of the LORD shall return, and come to Zion with songs and everlasting joy upon their heads: they shall obtain joy and gladness, and sorrow and sighing shall flee away.**

What a glorious time this will be. One can only imagine the many things that will be available to all the physical people who live and grow to know God and His righteous ways.

The physical people who remain as the kingdom is established will learn the ways of God and they will live in peace. Children will be born. People will live and die. During this time, the lake of fire will still be burning from the Battle of Armageddon. Those who choose not to live God's way, will be cast into it for their final punishment. Those who choose God's way will be changed and join the ranks of spiritual priests and kings that rule the earth with Christ.

There are over 69 references to the Kingdom of God in the New Testament. There are over 32 references to the Kingdom of Heaven in the New Testament. If you look the scriptures up with these phrases, you will see it is the gospel or good news Jesus came to preach.

[93]His disciples took the message to the world after His death. It is the ministry of Jesus when He came to earth the first time. It will be the ministry of the Two Witnesses when the Great Tribulation happens. It is what we must prepare for as Christians. The Kingdom of God on this earth will be a reality someday in the future. So says your bible.

THE SECOND RESURRECTION

> **Revelation 20:1-6**
>
> (1) And I saw an angel come down from heaven, having the key of the bottomless pit and a great chain in his hand.
>
> (2) And he laid hold on the dragon, that old serpent, which is the Devil, and Satan, and **bound him a thousand years,**
>
> (3) And cast him into the bottomless pit, and shut him up, and set a seal upon him, that he should deceive the nations no more, **till the thousand years should be fulfilled**: and after that he must be loosed a little season.
>
> (4) And I saw thrones, and they sat upon them, and judgment was given unto them: and *I saw* the souls of them that were beheaded for the witness of Jesus, and for the word of God, and which had not worshipped the beast, neither his image, neither had received *his* mark upon their foreheads, or in their hands; and **they lived and reigned with Christ a thousand years**.

(5) **But the rest of the dead lived not again until the thousand years were finished**. This *is* the first resurrection.

(6) Blessed and holy *is* he that hath part in the first resurrection: on such the second death hath no power, but they shall be priests of God and of Christ, and shall reign with him a thousand yrs.

This scripture is telling us there will be another resurrection of the people who have died down through history and were not in the first resurrection. This is where you must draw upon the Spirit of God to help you understand what this part of God's plan for all of humanity is about.

The key phrase is "*the rest of the dead*" lived not until the end of the 1,000 years.

Death is a touchy subject for most people. This is because of the different opinions about what happens after a person dies. To this discourse, we are dealing with judgment for the dead. We must return to the question asked in my first book, Why You Were Born.

[94]How do you get your name into the book of life? It is when you accept Jesus Christ into your life as head and leader of your life.

Well, what about all those people who lived and died before Jesus Christ was crucified for the sins of the world so we might receive eternal life? In ancient Israel God provided a ritual for the people to secure *physical salvation* from death when they sinned. It was by sacrificing a lamb or a goat…etc.

This is an important question for those and many who ignorantly do not accept Jesus' sacrifice for sin.

ONLY THE SACRIFICE OF JESUS CHRIST CAN SAVE YOU!

The bible is very plain about this:

Hebrews 10:1-18

(1) For the law having a shadow of good things to come, and not the very image of the things, ***can never with those sacrifices*** *which they offered year by year continually* ***make the comers thereunto perfect.***

(The animal sacrifices for sin were symbolic of the coming Lamb of God. It was **not yet time** in God's plan for these people to receive the Holy Spirit from God)

(2) For then would they not have ceased to be offered? because that the worshippers once purged should have had no more conscience of sins.

(3) But in those sacrifices there is a remembrance again made of sins every year.

(4) For it is not possible that the blood of bulls and of goats should take away sins.

(5) Wherefore when he cometh into the world, he saith, Sacrifice and offering you would not, but a body hast thou prepared me:

(6) In burnt offerings and sacrifices for sin thou have had no pleasure.

(7) Then said I, Lo, I come (in the volume of the book it is written of me,) to do thy will, O God.

---

[94]

(8) Above when he said, Sacrifice and offering and burnt offerings and offering for sin thou would not, neither have pleasure therein; which are offered by the law;

(9) Then said he, Lo, I come to do thy will, O God. <u>He taketh away the first</u>, that he may <u>establish the second</u>.

(10<u>) By the which will we are sanctified through the offering of the body of Jesus Christ once for all.</u>

(11) And every priest stands daily ministering and offering oftentimes the same sacrifices, which can never take away sins:

(12) <u>But this man,</u>(Jesus) <u>after he had offered one sacrifice for sins forever, sat down on the right hand of God;</u>

(13) From henceforth expecting till his enemies be made his footstool. (Psalms 110:1 Prophecy)

(14) For by one offering he hath perfected forever them that are sanctified.

(15) Whereof the Holy Spirit also is a witness to us: for after that he had said before,

(16) This is the covenant that I will make with them after those days, saith the Lord, I will put my laws into their hearts, and in their minds will I write them; (Jeremiah 31:31-33)

(17) **And their sins and iniquities will I remember no more**.

(18) Now where remission of these is, there is no more offering for sin.

The people who lived and died before Christ's fulfilled sacrifice for sin will be resurrected. That is what scripture says to me. How else could they have the opportunity that we have to be saved for eternity? <u>The only exception would be those who God dealt with individually before Christ</u>. I refer you to **Hebrews the 11th chapter** for the people of faith that are called out special to God.

There is a scripture in the Old Testament that is a prophecy that can help explain this second resurrection. God is talking about a time in the future when the **Whole House of Israel** would be raised up and given the opportunity to be saved.

Ezekiel 37:1-28

(1) The hand of the LORD was upon me, and carried me out in the spirit of the LORD, and set me down in the midst of the valley which *was* full of bones,

(2) And caused me to pass by them round about: and, behold, *there were* very many in the open valley; and, lo, *they were* very dry.

(3) And he said unto me, Son of man, can these bones live? And I answered, O Lord GOD, thou know.

(4) Again he said unto me, Prophesy upon these bones, and say unto them, O ye dry bones, hear the word of the LORD.

(5) Thus saith the Lord GOD unto these bones; Behold, I will cause breath to enter into you, and ye shall live:

(6) And I will lay sinews upon you, and will bring up flesh upon you, and cover you with skin, and put breath in you, and ye shall live; and ye shall know that I *am* the LORD.

(7) So I prophesied as I was commanded: and as I prophesied, there was a noise, and behold a shaking, and the bones came together, bone to his bone.

(8) And when I beheld, lo, the sinews and the flesh came up upon them, and the skin covered them above: but *there was* no breath in them.

(9) Then said he unto me, Prophesy unto the wind, prophesy, son of man, and say to the wind, Thus saith the Lord GOD; Come from the four winds, O breath, and breathe upon these slain, that they may live.

(10) So I prophesied as he commanded me, and the breath came into them, and they lived, and stood up upon their feet, an exceeding great army.

(11) **Then he said unto me, <u>Son of man, these bones are the whole house of Israel</u>:** (This has to be future; for David is dead and Israel is divided when this was written)behold, they say, Our bones are dried, and our hope is lost: we are cut off for our parts.

(12) Therefore prophesy and say unto them, Thus saith the Lord GOD; Behold, O my people, I will open your graves, and cause you to come up out of your graves, and bring you into the land of Israel.

(13) And ye shall know that I *am* the LORD, when I have opened your graves, O my people, and brought you up out of your graves,

(14) **<u>And shall put my spirit in you</u>, and ye shall live, and I shall place you in your own land: then shall ye know that I the LORD have spoken *it*, and performed *it*, saith the LORD.**

(15) The word of the LORD came again unto me, saying,

(16) Moreover, thou son of man, take thee one stick, and write upon it, For Judah, and for the children of Israel his companions: then take another stick, and write upon it, For Joseph, the stick of Ephraim, and *for* all the house of Israel his companions:

(17) And join them one to another into one stick; and they shall become one in thine hand.

(18) And when the children of thy people shall speak unto thee, saying, Wilt thou not shew us what thou *meanest* by these?

(19) Say unto them, Thus saith the Lord GOD; Behold, I will take <u>the stick of Joseph</u>, which *is* in the hand of Ephraim, and <u>the tribes of Israel his fellows</u>, and will put them with him, *even* with <u>the stick of Judah</u>, and **make them one stick**, and they shall be one in mine hand.

(20) And the sticks whereon thou write shall be in thine hand before their eyes.

(21) And say unto them, Thus saith the Lord GOD; Behold, I will take the children of Israel from among the heathen, whether they be gone, and will gather them on every side, and bring them into their own land:

(22) **And <u>I will make them one nation</u> in the land upon the mountains of Israel;** and one king shall be king to them all: and **<u>they shall be no more two nations</u>, neither shall they be <u>divided into two kingdoms any more at all</u>:**

(23) Neither shall they defile themselves any more with their idols, nor with their detestable things, nor with any of their transgressions: but I will save them out of all their dwelling places, wherein they have sinned, and will cleanse them: so shall they be my people, and I will be their God.

(24) **And <u>David my servant *shall be* king over them</u>;** and they all shall have one shepherd: they shall also walk in my judgments, and observe my statutes, and do them.

(25) And they shall dwell in the land that I have given unto Jacob my servant, wherein your fathers have dwelt; and they shall dwell therein, *even* they, and their children, and their children's children for ever: and **<u>my servant David *shall be* their prince forever.</u>**

(26) Moreover I will make a covenant of peace with them; it shall be an everlasting covenant with them: and I will place them, and multiply them, and will set my sanctuary in the midst of them for evermore.

(27) **My tabernacle also shall be with them: yea, I will be their God, and they shall be my people.**

(28) And the heathen shall know that I the LORD do sanctify Israel, when my sanctuary shall be in the midst of them for evermore.

There is little detail about this resurrection. One can only **speculate** what how and who will be involved. The plan of salvation suggests as I said, those who never had a chance to accept and follow Jesus will have that opportunity. They will also have the same atmosphere of evil to deal with. Notice that Satan will be set loose during this time.

I also <u>speculate</u> that the resurrections will be in 100-year phases over a period. Everyone who lived in a time slot of a 1,000 years. That way, those who were not as knowledgeable of the advancements of humanity would not be overwhelmed. If those people who lived during the time of Adam to Noah were raised with those during the time before Christ, there would be a huge information and knowledge gap. Who knows? Hopefully, we will be Spirit Beings serving Christ by that time.

There is a scripture that alludes to **100 years allotted for each person** to live during that time.

Isaiah 65:17-25

(17) For, behold, I create new heavens and a new earth: and the former shall not be remembered, nor come into mind. (*This sets the timeline for just before the Great White Throne Judgment when the earth will undergo a complete renewal by fire*)

(18) But be ye glad and rejoice forever *in that* which I create: for, behold, I create Jerusalem a rejoicing, and her people a joy.

(19) And I will rejoice in Jerusalem, and joy in my people: and the voice of weeping shall be no more heard in her, nor the voice of crying.

(20) <u>**There shall be no more thence an infant of days, nor an old man that hath not filled his days: for the child shall die an hundred years old; but the sinner *being* an hundred years old shall be accursed.**</u> (*This hints to a time when people will have 100 years from the time they are resurrected to make their choices in life. Some will be resurrected at the age they died I suppose for it says they will grow up and choose.*) (Also, the attitude is important; ***Matthew 19:14***

(14) But Jesus said, Suffer little children, and forbid them not, to come unto me: for of such is the kingdom of heaven.)

(21) And they shall build houses, and inhabit *them;* and they shall plant vineyards, and eat the fruit of them.

(22) They shall not build, and another inhabit; they shall not plant, and another eat: for as the days of a tree *are* the days of my people, and mine elect shall long enjoy the work of their hands.

(23) They shall not labor in vain, nor bring forth for trouble; for they *are* the seed of the blessed of the LORD, and their offspring with them.

(24) And it shall come to pass, that before they call, I will answer; and while they are yet speaking, I will hear.

(25) The wolf and the lamb shall feed together, and the lion shall eat straw like the bullock: and dust *shall be* the serpent's meat. They shall not hurt nor destroy in all my holy mountain, saith the LORD.

It will be a time of opportunity for those who did not have the choice of receiving Christ and the Holy Spirit to help them make choices in life.

Revelation 20:7-8

(7) And when the thousand years are expired, Satan shall be loosed out of his prison,

(8) And shall go out to deceive the nations which are in the four quarters of the earth, Gog and Magog, to gather them together to battle: the number of whom *is* as the sand of the sea.

The resurrected people will have to deal with many of the things we have to deal with in this world of evil and choices. The scriptures indicate there will be those who do not choose to comply with God and the established Kingdom. They will eventually become an army of evil and attack the people of God.

> **Revelation 20:9-10**
>
> (9) And they went up on the breadth of the earth, and compassed the camp of the saints about, and the beloved city: and fire came down from God out of heaven, and devoured them.
>
> (10) And **the devil that deceived them was cast into the lake of fire and brimstone**, where <u>the beast and the false prophet *were cast,* and shall be tormented day and night</u> for ever and ever.

It is not clear what this will accomplish. There is another scripture indicating that Satan and the demons will suffer a torment of some sort forever.

2Peter 2:4

(4) For if God spared not the angels that sinned, but cast *them* down **to hell**, and delivered *them* into chains of darkness, to be reserved unto judgment;

The English word hell in this verse is Tartaroo in the Greek, meaning an everlasting torment of darkness of some sort.

Scripture says fire consumed the people who came against the people of God's kingdom. Next comes the Great White Throne Judgment.

Revelation 20:11-15

(11) And I saw a great white throne, and Him that sat on it, from whose face the earth and the heaven fled away; and there was found no place for them. (The brightness and glory of God overpowers any light source)

(12) And I saw the dead, small and great, stand before God; and the books were opened: and **another book was opened**, which **is *the book* of life**: and the dead were judged out of those things which were written in the books, according to their works.

(13) And the sea gave up the dead which were in it; and death and hell delivered up the dead which were in them: and they were judged every man according to their works.

(14) And death and hell were cast into the lake of fire. This is the second death.

(15) And whosoever was not found written in the book of life was cast into the lake of fire.

A final judgment for all of humanity who ever lived. If your name is not in the Lamb's **"Book of Life"** you suffer the **"Second Death"** which is final punishment. Not torture, punishment. You are never to live again. In verse 14 when it says, *"cast into the lake of fire"*, I see this as when the fire spreads all over the earth at that time. (Speculation on my part) There is a scripture that alludes to this fact in the writings of Peter.

2Peter 3:10-13

(10) **But the day of the Lord** will come as a thief in the night; in the which the heavens shall pass away with a great noise, and the elements shall melt with fervent heat, **the earth also and the works that are therein shall be burned up.**

(11) *Seeing* then *that* all these things shall be dissolved, what manner *of persons* ought ye to be in *all* holy conversation and godliness,

(12) **Looking for and hasting unto the coming of the day of God, wherein the heavens being on fire shall be dissolved, and the elements shall melt with fervent heat?**

(13) Nevertheless we, according to his promise, **look for new heavens and a new earth, wherein dwelleth righteousness.**

This is the culmination of the **Day of the Lord** on earth.

Revelation 21:1

(1) And I saw a new heaven and a new earth: for the first heaven and the first earth were passed away; and **there was no more sea.**

A complete change of the earth's surface. Remember, at this time all evil is gone, and evil men are dead forever. This is now a planet of Spirit Beings, the children of the family of God.

The next thing John sees in vision is the Holy City.

THE HOLY CITY

Revelation 21:2-8

(2) And I John saw the holy city, new Jerusalem, coming down from God out of heaven, prepared as a bride adorned for her husband.

(3) And I heard a great voice out of heaven saying, Behold, the tabernacle of God *is* with men, and He will dwell with them, and they shall be His people, and **God himself shall be with them**, *and be* their God.

(4) And God shall wipe away all tears from their eyes; and **there shall be no more death**, neither sorrow, nor crying, neither shall there be any more pain: for the former things are passed away.

(5) And he that sat upon the throne said, **Behold, I make all things new**. And he said unto me, Write: for these words are true and faithful.

(6) And he said unto me, **It is done. I am Alpha and Omega, the beginning and the end**. I will give unto him that is athirst of the fountain of the water of life freely.

(7) He that overcomes shall inherit all things; and I will be his God, and he shall be my son.

(8) But *the fearful, and unbelieving*, and the abominable, and murderers, and whoremongers, and *sorcerers*, and *idolaters*, and *all liars*, shall have their part in the lake which burns with fire and brimstone: which is **the second death.**

This is the good news of what God has planned from the beginning. The creation of His spiritual family of beings. It is more than a human mind can contain in thought, it seems. Our potential is so much more than *"a halo and a rocking chair."*

When God is now making His dwelling with us in the Holy City that will come to rest on the spot where Jerusalem was.

This city will be 1,500 miles square. It will rise 1,500 miles into the sky. It will be filled with streets of Gold. There will be mansions for the saints to live and serve from. One can only imagine what God will do next, for His word does not tell us.

Revelation 21:9-27

(9) And there came unto me one of the seven angels which had the seven vials full of the seven last plagues, and talked with me, saying, Come hither, I will shew thee the bride, the Lamb's wife.

(10) And he carried me away in the spirit to a great and high mountain, and shewed me that great city, the holy Jerusalem, descending out of heaven from God,

(11) Having the glory of God: and her light *was* like unto a stone most precious, even like a jasper stone, clear as crystal;

(12) And had a wall great and high, *and* had twelve gates, and at the gates twelve angels, and names written thereon, which are *the names* of **the twelve tribes of the children of Israel**:

(13) On the east three gates; on the north three gates; on the south three gates; and on the west three gates.

(14) And the wall of the city had twelve foundations, and in them **the names of the twelve apostles of the Lamb.**

(15) And he that talked with me had a golden reed to measure the city, and the gates thereof, and the wall thereof.

(16) And the city lieth foursquare, and the length is as large as the breadth: and he measured the city with the reed, twelve thousand furlongs (*1,500 miles*). **The length and the breadth and the height of it are equal.**

(17) And he measured the wall thereof, an hundred *and* forty *and* four cubits, *according to* the measure of a man, that is, of the angel.

(18) And the building of the wall of it was *of* jasper: and **the city *was* pure gold, like unto clear glass.**

(19) **And the foundations of the wall of the city *were* garnished with all manner of precious stones**. The first foundation *was* jasper; the second, sapphire; the third, a chalcedony; the fourth, an emerald;

(20) The fifth, sardonyx; the sixth, sardius; the seventh, chrysolite; the eighth, beryl; the ninth, a topaz; the tenth, a chrysoprasus; the eleventh, a jacinth; the twelfth, an amethyst.

(21) And the twelve gates *were* twelve pearls; every several gate was of one pearl: and the street of the city *was* pure gold, as it were transparent glass.

(22) **And I saw no temple therein: for the Lord God Almighty and the Lamb are the temple of it.**

(23) And the city had no need of the sun, neither of the moon, to shine in it: for **the glory of God did lighten it, and the Lamb *is* the light thereof.**

(24) And the nations of them which are saved shall walk in the light of it: and the kings of the earth do bring their glory and honor into it.

(25) And the gates of it shall not be shut at all by day: for **there shall be no night there.**

(26) And they shall bring the glory and honor of the nations into it.

(27) And there shall in no wise enter into it anything that defiles, neither *whatsoever* worketh abomination, or *makes* a lie: **but they which are written in the Lamb's book of life.**

JESUS IS COMING

Revelation 22:6-21

(6) And he said unto me, These sayings *are* faithful and true: and the Lord God of the holy prophets sent his angel to shew unto his servants the things which must shortly be done.

(7) **Behold, I come quickly**: blessed *is* he that keeps the sayings of the prophecy of this book.

(8) And I John saw these things, and heard *them*. And when I had heard and seen, I fell down to worship before the feet of the angel which shewed me these things.

(9) Then saith he unto me, See *thou do it* not: for I am thy fellow servant, and of thy brethren the prophets, and of them which keep the sayings of this book: worship God.

(10) And he saith unto me, **Seal not** the sayings of the prophecy of this book: for the time is at hand.

(11) **He that is unjust, let him be unjust still: and he which is filthy, let him be filthy still: and he that is righteous, let him be righteous still: and he that is holy, let him be holy still.**

(12) And, behold, I come quickly; and my reward *is* with me, to give every man according as his work shall be.

(13) **I am Alpha and Omega, the beginning and the end, the first and the last.**

(14) **Blessed** *are* **they that do his commandments, that they may have right to the tree of life, and may enter in through the gates into the city.**

(15) For without *are* dogs, and sorcerers, and whoremongers, and murderers, and idolaters, and whosoever loveth and makes a lie.

(16) **I Jesus have sent mine angel to testify unto you these things in the churches.** I am the root and the offspring of David, *and* the bright and morning star.

(17) And the Spirit and the bride say, Come. And let him that heareth say, Come. And let him that is athirst come. And whosoever will, let him take the water of life freely.

(18) For I testify unto every man that heareth the words of the prophecy of this book, If any man shall add unto these things, God shall add unto him the plagues that are written in this book:

(19) And if any man shall take away from the words of the book of this prophecy, **God shall take away his part out of the book of life, and out of the holy city, and** *from* **the things which are written in this book.**

(20) **He which testifies these things saith, Surely I come quickly. Amen. Even so, come, Lord Jesus.**

(21) The grace of our Lord Jesus Christ *be* with you all. Amen.

BEYOND OUR IMANGINATION

The bible becomes silent about events after Jesus turns the kingdom over to the heavenly Father. The Father will move His throne to earth and the Holy City will come with it. Born of Spiritual essence; Children of God will occupy its many streets and mansions. Will it become the center of the universe? No one knows. But the bible certainly says that we humans are God's special creation. He is offering us potential to live forever with Him in this vast universe. Even if it were all a fairytale, it would be impressive. But it is not a fairytale! You must believe. Your belief begins with belief in Jesus Christ and God's plan for physical humanity to become literal born spirit beings into God's very family of spirit beings! Will you make the choices that are needed for you to be there when God opens your mind to see and believe His plan for you?

"The grace of our Lord Jesus Christ *be* with you all. Amen."
THE END

www.ingramcontent.com/pod-product-compliance
Lightning Source LLC
LaVergne TN
LVHW041705060526
838201LV00043B/582